"This book is your invitati[...] Why not take this opportunity to respond to [...] listen, to love, to follow, to risk, and to live for what matters most. It is never too late to let Jesus change us from the inside out."

BLAND MASON, Pastor, City on a Hill Church, Boston, MA;
Chaplain, Boston Red Sox

"Every Christian understands weakness and failure. Dan's latest book is a powerful reminder that Jesus stands ready to forgive us when we fall. Pick up this book—you'll find encouragement to love Jesus more."

FLAME, Grammy- and Dove-nominated Christian Hip-hop Artist

"This is more substantial and of longer-lasting value than any power breakfast I know. I found Dan's book current, relevant, and life-changing."

LOREN RENO, Lt. Gen., USAF (Ret.);
Author, *10 Leadership Maneuvers: A General's Guide to Serving and Leading*

"Dan is a great communicator who knows how to apply the gospel powerfully and insightfully to ordinary people's lives. His ministry with college students gives him a unique window into what is happening in the culture at large, and how the gospel speaks to questions both new and old. *Sunny Side Up* is Dan at his best!"

J.D. GREEAR, Pastor, The Summit Church, Raleigh-Durham, NC;
President, Southern Baptist Convention

"What an invitation the risen Jesus gives Peter on that beach in Galilee— 'Come and have breakfast'; and what a call he then issues—'Come, follow me!' As Dan DeWitt says, if we take this breakfast conversation to heart, it can radically change our lives."

RICO TICE, Senior Minister (Evangelism), All Souls, Langham Place, London;
Founder, Christianity Explored Ministries

"What a great little book! It is profound and challenging but also joyfully optimistic. It didn't just tell me to follow Jesus; it helped me want to. This will really help anyone who is trying to work out what following Jesus actually means."

JONTY ALLCOCK, Co-pastor, Globe Church, London;
Author, *Lost*; *Hero;* and *Fearless*

"Dan DeWitt has produced a great book! It is straightforward and funny, and pulls no punches as it walks us through Jesus' breakfast with his friend Peter. Read it yourself, and then read it with a mate—it will do both of you real good!"

GARY MILLAR, Principal, Queensland Theological College

"Simple but solid. Pithy but profound. Conversational but convicting. Whether you're new on the faith journey or far down the road, you'll find this little book challenging and encouraging."

JOHN D. STRAIN, Chaplain, The Pines, Whiting, NJ

"We're convinced meaningful relationships are often shaped over meals. Dan DeWitt's fresh take on Peter's breakfast with Jesus is both insightful and inspiring. It's refreshing and restorative."

D.A. AND ELICIA HORTON, Co-authors, *Enter the Ring*

"*Sunny Side Up* is as encouraging as it is challenging. This is the kind of book that makes you want to get off the bench and get in the game. Dan reminds us that Jesus is calling us to follow him in love. And Jesus loves us enough to give us all the grace we need to do so."

ERIC IVERSON, Executive Director, Youth Leadership, Minneapolis, MN

"One of the biggest battles of the Christian life is the fight to keep our relationship with God from becoming routine. With *Sunny Side Up*, Dan DeWitt challenges us to wake up and rediscover our first love. It's a challenge to put Jesus and his church back in first place in our lives. If you need to reprioritize, here is your how-to guide. This is a breakfast you won't want to skip."

KEVIN EZELL, President, North American Mission Board, SBC

"Read this book and then live the rest of your life practicing what Peter learned: that loving our Redeemer makes obedience more desirable and provides a real center of gravity for our lives in him."

MIGUEL NÚÑEZ, Senior Pastor, International Baptist Church, Santo Domingo; President, Wisdom and Integrity Ministries

SUNNY SIDE UP

the good book
COMPANY

Dedicated to Gregg and Anna McMullen:
godparents to our children and the truest friends the
DeWitt family has ever known. We love you guys.

Sunny Side Up
© 2019, Daniel DeWitt.

Published by
The Good Book Company
Tel (UK): 0333 123 0880
International: +44 (0) 208 942 0880
Email: info@thegoodbook.co.uk

Websites:
North America: www.thegoodbook.com
UK: www.thegoodbook.co.uk
Australia: www.thegoodbook.com.au
New Zealand: www.thegoodbook.co.nz

Cover design by Dan DeWitt. Design and art direction by André Parker

ISBN: 9781784982942 | Printed in the UK

CONTENTS

FOREWORD BY KYLE IDLEMAN

AUTHOR, *NOT A FAN* AND *DON'T GIVE UP*

I love mornings, and I love breakfast. For me, a morning breakfast meeting with Jesus and his people is the perfect way to start the day off right. I have two or three breakfast spots I frequent often. Eggs over easy and chicken sausage with a side of avocado is usually in order—I need that avocado; it's a fruit, you know. But more than the food, it's the conversations that are most enjoyable and impactful.

At breakfast, decisions are made, perspectives solidified, visions cast, and intentions set. And, although I love to influence and be influenced by other Christians over breakfast, it's my morning breakfast appointments with Jesus and his word that are always the most enduring.

Reading, studying, writing, praying—with a side of listening to Jesus—always make for a life-changing morning. When I humble myself and hear from him, my mind is renewed and my heart impassioned. When

I drop the pressures and confess my mistakes, my life is restored and my path becomes clear.

In this inspiring read, my brother Dan DeWitt replays the most important breakfast of the disciple Peter's life. Jesus often used mealtimes to call and influence his followers. This particular morning meal that Jesus shared with Peter, recorded in John's Gospel, is filled with hope for you and me. It can change our lives if we let it.

Jesus offers Peter forgiveness when he desperately needs it, and knows he doesn't deserve it. That's what Jesus does. With compassion and grace, yet holding Peter accountable, Jesus offers a path forward, a renewed life. He calls Peter to a deeper commitment and greater sacrifice.

In Peter's moments with Jesus, he is broken and repentant. He surrenders. He submits to Jesus again. And Jesus is there to receive him. In this moment, Peter really goes from acting like a fan of Jesus, someone who trails from a distance, to being a faithful follower of Jesus.

In the book *Not a Fan*, I share what it takes to become a completely committed follower of Jesus. It's not an easy message, although it's quite simple. Perhaps Jesus shares it best in Luke 9:

> *Whoever wants to be my disciple must deny themselves and take up their cross daily and follow me.*
>
> *(Luke 9 v 23)*

This is a tough teaching. It's a challenging message. But it's for everyone who would follow Jesus. For many, it's just too much. So often we much prefer to simply be "fans" of Jesus, rather than completely devoted. But Jesus doesn't call us to be fans. He calls us to be followers.

I believe that the biggest threat to the church today is fans who call themselves Christians but aren't actually interested in following Christ. They want to be close enough to Jesus to get all the benefits, but not so close that it requires everything from them.

Jesus has a lot of fans these days. Fans who cheer for him when things are going well, but who walk away when life gets difficult. Fans who sit safely in the stands cheering, but who know nothing of sacrifice on the field. Fans of Jesus who know all about him but don't *know* him.

But Jesus was never interested in having fans. When he defines what kind of relationship he wants, "enthusiastic admirer" isn't an option.

Jesus makes it clear: "Whoever wants to be my disciple must deny themselves and take up their cross daily and follow me."

We see this in Peter's life. When Jesus was arrested, Peter followed him from a distance. Peter wanted to be close enough to see what was going on but not too close. And when he had no escape, when confronted with the question "Aren't you one of Jesus' disciples?" he responded, "No! I don't know him!" Peter was a fair-weather fan.

But Jesus didn't leave Peter in his failure. As Dan shares, Jesus offered Peter the forgiveness of a lifetime over a campfire at sunrise. The story of Peter's life-changing breakfast meeting will challenge you too to quit playing games and grow in your commitment as a forgiven follower of Jesus.

For some, this book will be a wake-up call. For others, it will be like an invitation you responded to years ago. For all, it will serve as the start of a new day—a new day to deny yourself and follow Jesus.

Friends, as I am sharing this with you, I am reminding myself, *Never eat breakfast alone*. You should invite Jesus to every breakfast—when you are by yourself or with others. Welcome him, and you will experience his life-changing presence.

Thank you, Dan, for this message.

Kyle Idleman

INTRO:
THE MOST IMPORTANT
MEAL OF THE DAY

Early in the morning, Jesus stood on the shore, but the
disciples did not realize that it was Jesus.
(John 21 v 4)

You start every morning with your normal routine. Your alarm clock goes off and you face your first important decision of the day: to snooze or not to snooze. No matter how many times you hit it, you know you eventually have to brave the day. So, you finally roll out of bed on autopilot.

Shower. Dress. Coffee. Another day.

Life can feel mundane at times, can't it? But what if today was different? What if this morning you had a breakfast conversation that changed the direction of your life? It's happened for others before. Why not you? Why not now?

BACON WITH A SIDE OF GRACE

Imagine if you had the chance to meet a world-renowned leader you respect. Take your pick. Who would it be? What do you think they would tell you? Do you think it would have any impact on your day? Your life?

They say—whoever *they* are—that breakfast is the most important meal of the day. If that's true, then a bunch us are in trouble. A lot of us tend to skip breakfast. Sometimes we skip other important stuff too. Maybe that's why life can sometimes feel a bit ordinary. Maybe we're missing something.

But what if that changed?

If you had your pick of leadership gurus to learn from over breakfast, you'd probably get up earlier than normal to head off to your restaurant of choice. I understand that if you're not a morning person, this might be a little hard to imagine. But try.

Just picture yourself backing out of your driveway to head to your favorite café, pub, or diner. It's a once-in-a-lifetime kind of thing. You turn left off Main Street into a faded asphalt parking lot. The yellow stripes are nearly gone, yet folks still manage to line up in rows.

As soon as you step out of your car, the smell of fresh bacon greets you and guides you across the parking lot. You pull open the glass door with a steel bar handle, clanging the "We're open" sign and ringing a rusty bell that's as old as the restaurant. The sound of busy servers and a dozen conversations welcomes you inside. "Mornin' sweetheart," a middle-aged woman says, as she directs you to a booth and sets a laminate menu on the table in front of you. To go with the bacon, there are eggs any way you want them: scrambled, over-easy, sunny side up…

She quickly returns with utensils wrapped in a white napkin and a green coffee mug that's branded with a yellow John Deere logo. Steam drifts upwards as she fills your cup from her stainless-steel decanter with a brown spout. No decaf for you. You want to be wide-awake for this.

But what if the person you're meeting isn't merely a successful entrepreneur or a talented leader but the Creator of the world? I know it might sound far-fetched, but it really isn't. It's happened before. In the last chapter of John's Gospel we read that Jesus had breakfast with the disciple Peter before saying his final words and going back to heaven.

And, let's be honest, Peter was an idiot. He had just blown it big time. He had flat out denied three times that he even knew who Jesus was. He struck out cold. But still, Jesus had breakfast with him. And it changed Peter's life.

Like Peter, we can all be idiots at some time or another. I know I am. The good news is that Jesus makes time for idiots like us. And he's still in the business of changing lives.

He can change yours. He can change mine. If life's a struggle at the moment, Jesus can change it for the better. And even if life's pretty good, I guarantee he can bring deeper satisfaction and greater joy than you could imagine. It can start this morning, even over breakfast.

A GALILEAN ACCENT

In the following chapters we're going to immerse ourselves in a conversation that Jesus had two thousand years ago on the shores of the Sea of Galilee, where a group of silhouetted men, including Peter, sat around a fire at sunrise enjoying a morning meal. It's found in the last chapter of John's Gospel.

So, grab your Bible and a cup of coffee. Maybe you'll even want to read through this little book while you're sitting in your favorite breakfast spot—that would seem appropriate. But regardless of where you read this, or what chapter of life this finds you in, I pray that the Spirit of God would speak to you through the inspired words of Scripture.

Because whenever Jesus speaks, there is no telling what might happen. If you start your day with him, who knows where it might end. And maybe, just maybe—in the midst of all the voices in the coffee shop or breakfast joint—maybe you will hear a voice with a Galilean accent calling you to stop, and sit, and listen. And be changed.

JOHN 21 v 1-25

Afterward Jesus appeared again to his disciples, by the Sea of Galilee. It happened this way: Simon Peter, Thomas (also known as Didymus), Nathanael from Cana in Galilee, the sons of Zebedee, and two other disciples were together. "I'm going out to fish," Simon Peter told them, and they said, "We'll go with you." So they went out and got into the boat, but that night they caught nothing.

Early in the morning, Jesus stood on the shore, but the disciples did not realize that it was Jesus.

He called out to them, "Friends, haven't you any fish?"

"No," they answered.

He said, "Throw your net on the right side of the boat and you will find some." When they did, they were unable to haul the net in because of the large number of fish.

Then the disciple whom Jesus loved said to Peter, "It is the Lord!" As soon as Simon Peter heard him say, "It is the Lord," he wrapped his outer garment around him (for he had taken it off) and jumped into the water. The other disciples followed in the boat, towing the net full of fish, for they were not far from shore, about a hundred yards. When they landed, they saw a fire of burning coals there with fish on it, and some bread.

Jesus said to them, "Bring some of the fish you have just caught." So Simon Peter climbed back into the boat and dragged the net ashore. It was full of large fish, 153, but even with so many the net was not torn. Jesus said to them, "Come and have breakfast." None of the disciples dared ask him, "Who are you?" They knew it was the Lord. Jesus came, took the bread and gave it to them, and did the same with the fish. This was now the third time Jesus appeared to his disciples after he was raised from the dead.

When they had finished eating, Jesus said to Simon Peter, "Simon son of John, do you love me more than these?"

"Yes, Lord," he said, "you know that I love you."

Jesus said, "Feed my lambs."

Again Jesus said, "Simon son of John, do you love me?"

He answered, "Yes, Lord, you know that I love you."

Jesus said, "Take care of my sheep."

The third time he said to him, "Simon son of John, do you love me?"

Peter was hurt because Jesus asked him the third time, "Do you love me?" He said, "Lord, you know all things; you know that I love you."

Jesus said, "Feed my sheep. Very truly I tell you, when you were younger you dressed yourself and went where you wanted; but when you are old you will stretch out your hands, and someone else will dress you and lead you where you do not want to go." Jesus said this to indicate the kind of death by which Peter would glorify God. Then he said to him, "Follow me!"

Peter turned and saw that the disciple whom Jesus loved was following them. (This was the one who had leaned back against Jesus at the supper and had said, "Lord, who is going to betray you?") When Peter saw him, he asked, "Lord, what about him?"

Jesus answered, "If I want him to remain alive until I return, what is that to you? You must follow me." Because of this, the rumor spread among the believers that this disciple would not die. But Jesus did not say that he would not die; he only said, "If I want him to remain alive until I return, what is that to you?"

This is the disciple who testifies to these things and who wrote them down. We know that his testimony is true.

Jesus did many other things as well. If every one of them were written down, I suppose that even the whole world would not have room for the books that would be written.

1. HEART-HEALTHY OPTIONS

Again Jesus said, "Simon son of John, do you love me?"
(John 21 v 16)

It was a day when nothing happened and everything changed. I was listening to an old-fashioned, hellfire-and-brimstone preacher. He was loud. He was pacing back and forth in front of hundreds of students at a youth camp, talking about what it means to be a follower of Jesus. I was captivated.

I'd only been a Christian for about twenty-four hours. The evening service the night before was when it first made sense to me. That's when I believed the gospel message and received God's love and forgiveness offered through Jesus Christ. This night's talk was about how followers of Jesus need to love him with their whole heart.

The speaker's final challenge to all the campers was to find somewhere after the service to spend time in prayer. He told us to stay there until we loved God with our whole heart. I was sincere, passionate, and naïve. I couldn't wait to try.

This youth camp had all the bells and whistles, by the way. They had bowling. They had a "snack shack" where you could get a cheeseburger and a milkshake. They had putt-putt golf. They had basketball courts. And after the service that's where everyone seemed to scatter. After the last "Amen," it was youth camp party time.

I remember standing there watching everyone walk away and thinking, *"But the preacher told us to go find some quiet place to tell God we love him?!"* I had only followed Jesus for one day and already I had become judgmental. I'm a natural-born Pharisee, I suppose.

To give myself a little credit—which is the proper Pharisee thing to do—I didn't think about it too long. I was intent on walking out into the woods and trying this whole thing out.

I found a nice quiet spot where I knelt between some bushes. I placed my hands on the ground in front of me and rested my forehead on my hands.

I prayed over and over, "Dear God, I want to love you with all my heart." When nothing magical happened, I began emphasizing each word: "DEAR God, I want to love you... Dear GOD, I want to love you..." Still nothing.

I was hoping for the miraculous. I was thinking the bushes might catch on fire and that I'd hear a deep voice, like that of actor Morgan Freeman, saying, "Yes, Dan, you now love me with all of your heart. You can go play putt-putt and get a cheeseburger now."

Still nothing.

After what seemed like hours, I finally stopped praying. I was only fifteen years old at the time, and I bet I didn't pray for more than fifteen minutes. But it seemed like a really long time to my adolescent self. To be honest, back then it felt like a whole lot of nothing. I was a bit disappointed.

A TOTAL ECLIPSE OF THE HEART

Those first two days of my Christian life sum up how it can be for many of us. Sometimes we are wholehearted about living for God. Other times our hearts are elsewhere—whether we're proud and judgmental, as I was that evening, or simply focused on other aspects of our busy lives. Other things can easily eclipse our love for God.

I wonder what you see as you look back? Was there a time when you felt you knew and loved God more than you do now? When you were wholehearted about following Jesus? Or maybe you've never been sure that level of commitment is really for you? Maybe your Christian life has been a bit like an oscillating fan turning back and forth; one minute you're focused on loving God and the next distracted by other things.

I sometimes laugh, thinking back to that event at youth camp. But I realize that I understood then something I often miss now. *Jesus wants my heart above everything else.* It was true of me then. It was true for Peter 2000 years ago. And it's true for each one of us right now. Jesus wants your *heart*.

Maybe you think focusing on your heart sounds a bit silly. But the truth is, God wants to develop in you the kind of heart and attitude that were in Jesus. That's at the top of his agenda. His powerful love can transform us and guide us to follow in his steps: "This is how we know what love is: Jesus Christ laid down his life for us. And we ought to lay down our lives for our brothers and sisters" (1 John 3 v 16).

BELIEVING IN GOD ISN'T ENOUGH

Orthodoxy may sound like a painfully expensive dental procedure, but it really means having proper beliefs about God. Orthodoxy is where every person must begin in their relationship with God. That's not to say people have to pass a test about the Bible in order to become a Christian. Thankfully, God isn't looking for academic qualifications or good grades. But in order to become a follower of Jesus, you have to have a right understanding of who Jesus is and the forgiveness he offers.

Growing in our relationship with God doesn't involve less than orthodoxy. But it certainly involves more. You can have right beliefs but still develop the wrong kind of heart toward God. It's possible to become a cold, religious person. That's not God's plan for you. God wants your heart.

It's even possible for an entire church to miss the mark when it comes to loving God. Here's how the apostle John reports Jesus' words about the church in Ephesus, who were known for their orthodoxy. Their problem wasn't truth. They were good at truth. But they had grown cold in their love for God:

> *I know your deeds, your hard work and your perseverance. I know that you cannot tolerate wicked people, that you have tested those who claim to be apostles but are not, and have found them false. You have persevered and have endured hardships for my name, and have not grown weary. Yet I hold this against you:* **You have forsaken the love you had at first.** *Consider how far you have fallen!*   (Revelation 2 v 2-5)

This church in Ephesus had got the truth right but had then lost its first love. That can happen to individuals too. Has it happened to you?

A relationship with Jesus begins with truth, with orthodoxy, with forming the proper beliefs about who Jesus really is. This is illustrated in one of the key defining moments in the life of the disciples, when Jesus asked them what they believed about him. They volleyed around some of the more generous titles overheard in the villages they'd visited: John the Baptist, Elijah, or maybe some other prophet (Mark 8 v 27-29). But then

Jesus made the question more personal and asked what they believed about *him*.

Peter spoke up right away. He did that a lot. "You're the Messiah," Peter declared. This is where Peter got an A on his orthodoxy test. And since we're going to pick on Peter a bit in this book, it's only appropriate that we celebrate his successes here. Bravo Peter! You're one orthodox dude. Well done!

But in the last chapter of John's Gospel, we don't find Jesus questioning Peter's beliefs or orthodoxy, do we? We might think it would make sense if he did. After all, in the opening of Acts, Peter is about to preach the historic sermon where God launches the church. Three thousand captivated people will decide to follow Jesus in response to Peter's sermon (Acts 2 v 14-41). So it's important that Peter gets it right.

(Warning: Technical language used by nerdy Bible-college professors follows. Don't worry. I'll try to explain what the nerdy words mean.)

It would make sense if Jesus asked Peter about his *theology* (beliefs about God) or his *Christology* (beliefs about Christ) or his *eschatology* (beliefs about the end of human history).

Nope.

That's not what Jesus talked to Peter about on the shore that morning. Peter would go on to play a massive role for thousands of people who would decide to follow Jesus. That's why you might think Jesus would ask about his *ecclesiology* (beliefs about the church). But that's not what Jesus had in store for their seaside conversation.

So, now we've gotten all the technical terms out of the way, let's focus on what Jesus *did* ask Peter. He asked him about his love. He asked about his heart. That points us to what really matters to God, doesn't it?

You see, orthodoxy—proper beliefs—is where we begin. We can't grow very much in our love for God without also growing in our beliefs about God. What we believe about God is vitally important.

But orthodoxy is not where we end. It's dangerously possible to grow in our *knowledge* of God without growing in our *love* for God. We can accumulate a lot of knowledge while our hearts remain far from him.

Jesus said that loving God with all of our heart is the greatest command (Mark 12 v 30-31). That should make us stop and think. Since Jesus calls it the greatest command, it must matter a lot.

Maybe we need to reclaim that little word "love", because it can sound a bit tame, soft, or even soppy. Love is what motivates people to die to save their families or protect their countries. And love is why Jesus died to save us. There's nothing weak about that kind of love.

Think for a moment about how you use the word "love". Who would you say, "I love you," to? Your wife? Your child? Your mom? What else would you say you love? A sports team? A band? Your dog? All of these loves differ, but none of them quite match up to the kind of love the Lord asks of us.

Loving God isn't a flowers-and-chocolates kind of love. Neither is it cheering him on from the sidelines or singing his latest hit. God wants your heart—and he wants all of it.

CONFESSIONS OF A DIVINITY MASTER

If you came to my office, you'd see some degrees on my wall. They're all nicely framed. You might even be mildly impressed.

I have one degree that really is impressive, in my humble but accurate opinion. It's called a Master of Divinity. I, the one writing these words on this page, am a Master of Divinity!

A quick Google search shows that "divinity" is a hotly contested concept. It either means the "state or quality of being divine" or a "fluffy, creamy candy made with stiffly beaten egg whites." So, I've either mastered the art of being divine or I'm a sweet and fluffy treat. Decide for yourself.

It really means I've taken a bunch of classes about the Bible and God. And I have the degree to prove it. Divinity has been mastered by yours truly.

How impressed is God with the degrees hanging on my wall? I'd bet all the money in my pockets against all the money in your pockets that the answer is not very much. To be honest, I imagine he was more impressed with the fifteen-year-old boy who just wanted to love him with all his heart.

On that day so long ago, it felt as if nothing happened. But I was doing my best to love God. And that isn't nothing. It's something. In fact, it's what it's all about.

GROWING OR WITHERING?

Accomplishments and successes are not substitutes for growing in our love for God.

Anyone who has begun a relationship with God understands the powerful impulse to give God our whole lives, our whole heart. But it's an impulse that has to be nurtured and fed in order to grow. There's a whole lot in life that threatens our love for God.

It's not always a massive sin issue that deters our growth. Sometimes it's just being distracted with our lives, careers, families, hobbies, and responsibilities. Our love for God can easily get squeezed out of the position of priority it deserves. Productivity can become an enemy of what matters most.

Is life like that for you? If so, I get it. I like to have a lot of projects going and I like to be productive. But sometimes just doing more isn't the answer.

Being more productive might not produce more happiness in your life. Being more successful might take you further from what is most important and nearer to true failure. You could be going in the wrong direction.

And if you're going in the wrong direction, do you really think speeding up is going to help?

Jesus said it this way: "What good is it for someone to gain the whole world, yet forfeit their soul?" (Mark 8 v 36). That means you can gain everything and still lose in the end. You can win the world at the expense of what matters most. Maybe it's time to stop long enough to think about what matters most.

Don't spend your life climbing to the top of a three-rung ladder. You were created for something real, something powerful, something soul-satisfying, something *more*. You were created to know and love God.

I know that slowing down to think about it might not come easy. For some, it might even expose a dark secret. Your activity and ambition could be a distraction to keep you from asking tough questions. You might be hiding behind your calendar.

Have you ever considered what fills your empty thoughts? The answer to that question will likely reveal what God wants to work on in your life right now. The answer will expose what has most captivated your affections. What you care about most will drive and dominate your life.

That's why God wants your heart, plain and simple. That's what Jesus was after with Peter. That's what he's after with you.

So if we want to love God more, where do we start? We only grow in love for someone as we get to know them and spend time with them. One practical thing you can do is to make sure you have some quiet time each day to focus on your relationship with God through reading the Bible and spending time in prayer. You can start by reading through the Gospel of John.

Maybe you've done something like this before. Maybe not. We've included a one-month reading plan in the back of this book to get you started. Read a passage of the Bible each day. (There are plenty of Bible apps that offer you the convenience of reading a digital copy on your phone.) Spend a few moments reflecting on what you've read and respond to God in prayer.

Spending time with God is vitally important to growing in our love for him. Love is what matters most. The apostle Paul goes so far as to say that we can perform miracles and even die as martyrs, but it is all meaningless if we don't have love (1 Corinthians 13). That's because love is at the center of God's work in the world.

ON WHY WE'RE NOT CYBORGS

In the beginning God made two humans, Adam and Eve, and placed them in a perfect setting, the Garden of Eden. But why did God make them? And why did he make them with the capacity for rebellion?

He could have made them like cyborgs that robotically kept all his commands. They could have been perfectly programmed to always obey. They could have been designed to never botch things and get us all kicked out of paradise. That would have been nice. Or would it?

Instead, God made this man and this woman with the mysterious ability to *choose*. It's almost as if this ability to decide—this freedom to love or hate, to worship or slander—was fundamental to his design. While it can be hard to unpack exactly how all of this works in the Bible, one thing seems clear: God wants us to love him and has made a world, and worked within this world, to make it possible for us to do so.

I think that humanity would not have the ability to love if rebellion were not also a possibility. I've heard Christian teacher Professor John Lennox make this point with an illustration from parenting. Though every analogy is limited, I find this one helpful. When parents have children, Lennox explains, they hope their kids will grow up to love them. But there is always the real risk the opposite might happen. Their children might turn away and rebel. They might grow up to hate their parents.

Parents indeed take a great risk by having children. It seems God was willing to do something similar. But since God knows the end from the beginning, he knew exactly what was going to happen and what the cost would be. Still, knowing all that, God created us to love him. But we can also reject him if we so desire. This is the most important decision we can ever make. It's not a choice we should take lightly.

If we choose to love God properly, so many other things will fall into place. I don't mean life will become problem free. Nor do I mean that we can somehow perfect our love for God in this life. But we can ask him to help us keep growing in our knowledge and love of him, right up to the day we have the joy of seeing him face to face.

With God's help, even in the midst of all our imperfections, we can still develop attitudes and actions that please him. Wonderfully, we please God when we worship him and seek to grow in our love for and knowledge of him. I think I pleased God at the age of fifteen bowing before him in the midst of some bushes out in the woods at a youth camp.

Come to think of it, those bushes were probably the cause of my horrible poison-ivy breakout that summer. But all itching aside, my point is that even on our best day, none of us deserve God's love. We are beggars, every one of us. Love is the only proper response to such undeserved grace. And growing in this love is at the center of the Christian life.

OVER TO YOU

So, how are you responding to God's love? Have you let your love grow cold? Are you like the church at Ephesus, good at truth but cold in love? Are you more focused on being busy for God (or for yourself) than on growing in your love for him? Is there a sin issue in your life that is holding you back?

Think carefully about your life. The first part of this breakfast conversation between Jesus and Peter is foundational. Our heart toward God sets the stage for everything that follows. If we take this seriously, it can dramatically change our lives. That's because what captures your affection will demand your devotion and determine your life direction.

So, let me ask you, can you remember a time in your life when you loved Jesus more than you do today? If you do, what happened? Are you ready to return to the love you first had for God?

No matter who you are, or where you are, you can get in on the invitation to love God. God desires and demands our full affection. That's because he is the greatest good. And his invitation to love him is for our greatest good. Loving God is what's best for us.

That's because this world's not going to satisfy us. We can win it all and still lose everything. We were made for more. So, let's turn our hearts to him. He alone can fill our lives with the meaning and purpose we've unsuccessfully tried to find elsewhere.

You may feel that you're a million miles away, too far to turn back to your first love. I'm sure Peter felt like that on the morning Jesus found him fishing. But you will find God waiting for you the moment you turn around. After all, he's never far from any of us (Acts 17 v 27).

Maybe you need to seek out a nice quiet place where you can get alone with God and tell him that you want to grow in your love for him. You can even go out in the woods like I did; just watch out for the poison ivy. Tell God you're sorry for whatever it is that has kept you from growing. Ask him for the grace to grow in wisdom, obedience, and love.

There probably won't be a burning bush or a deep voice booming down from heaven. You might even feel that nothing is happening at all. But God is always pleased to see his children run to him.

Just look at this breakfast conversation between Jesus and Peter in John 21. This isn't some weird, sentimental love fest. This is a man who had just died on a bloody cross, and then walked out of an empty tomb after trampling over death and the grave, showing another man the kind of love that is worthy of the greatest kind of sacrifice.

Before he returned to heaven, Jesus stopped long enough to give Peter the chance to say, "I love you Lord."

It's your turn now.

2. FINDING OUR PLACE AT THE TABLE

"Do you love me more than these?"
(John 21 v 15)

Peter seems like the kind of guy who wore his virtues and his vices on his sleeve. You probably wouldn't have to wonder what Peter was thinking or feeling. He'd let you know.

I imagine if all of Peter's secrets were made public, there wouldn't be many surprises. His stuff was all front and center. Most of us are probably a bit more insulated, more guarded, than that. Not Peter. If it was on his mind, it would quickly find its way out of his mouth.

As we saw in the last chapter, Jesus is getting at Peter's heart in this breakfast conversation. Jesus asks Peter three times if he loves him. But one question is curiously different than the other two. The first time, Jesus says, "Do you love me *more than these*?"

Jesus never said anything without reason, so what is the "more than these" he is talking about? And what difference should it make in our lives? As you'll see, there are a few options as to what these words mean—and get ready to be challenged, because they all have powerful personal applications that can transform our lives. If we take them seriously, none of us can get past Jesus' words unscathed.

THREE OPTIONS

I remember telling my wife that I wished we had a video Bible so that we'd know what Jesus was talking about in this verse. After all, I'm sure it was obvious to Peter what Jesus meant by "more than these." Maybe Jesus looked directly at whatever he was talking about, or even pointed at them, his eyes or fingers showing Peter what he meant.

So when we got an animated Bible-story video for our kids, I was thrilled that it included this scene from John 21. I called upstairs to my wife, "April, you've got to come down and see this!" Just as I imagined, in the cartoon version Jesus clearly points to something. "Eureka! That's it! That's what Jesus meant," I told my wife as our small children stared back in confusion. They had never seen me get that excited about one of their cartoons.

Of course, like us, the makers of the video were just doing their best to figure out what Jesus meant. They had to decide what Jesus was going to point to using the same evidence we will use. In my opinion there are three good options for understanding what Jesus meant when he said, "*more than these*".

1. Do you love me *more than these other things that you love*?

2. Do you love me *more than you love these other people*?

3. Do you love me *more than these others love me*?

And in all three we'll find a disruptive challenge waiting...

OPTION ONE: GONE FISHING

First, the *more than these* could refer to fishing. Peter loved to fish. That's where Jesus found him on this morning.

You get the sense reading the Gospels that every time Jesus turned around, Peter would duck out the back and head to the sea. It's kind of like the country music song where a woman gives her husband an ultimatum: it's either her or fishing. The man's choice becomes clear as he sings that he's going to miss her but the fish are biting just fine. The fish win.

But for Peter, fishing was more than just a hobby. It was his career. It was his livelihood. And if he was like most men, this was probably where he found a lot of his identity and self-worth.

Jesus could be saying to Peter, *Do you love me more than fishing boats and nets, more than all of the stuff that makes up your career?* Or he could be saying, *Peter, am I what defines your identity? Is our relationship where you find your basis for self-worth?* This interpretation of "more than these" certainly provides a powerful application that we should all take to heart. We should find our identity and self-worth in our relationship with Jesus. But that can be easier said than done.

Think for a moment about your own life. If you work, how would you feel if you lost your job? Or if injury meant you couldn't play your favorite sport? Or if a social group you're involved with stopped running? Imagine how that might affect your identity and self-worth.

If you'd find any of these things devastating, what might that say about where you're basing your sense of identity? Think about what it would take to relocate the center of your identity to your relationship with God. How would that affect those other areas of your life? Jesus wants to be the main defining characteristic of your identity. What would have to change in your life for that to happen?

OPTION TWO: GOOD FELLAS

Second, Jesus could be talking about the disciples. Peter was fishing with them that morning. In John 21 we find Peter sitting in his underwear in a boat with the other disciples. Guys can be weird, can't they?

When they hear Jesus on the beach, Peter quickly puts his outer garments back on. That makes perfect sense since he then dives in the water, fully clothed, and swims to Jesus. Guys can be weird, can't they?

So when Jesus asked, "Do you love me more than these?" he could be getting at the source of Peter's community. Did Peter love Jesus more than he loved the other disciples? Did Peter find his ultimate acceptance in human relationships or in his relationship with Jesus, the Son of God?

Jesus could be saying, *Peter, do you love me more than your small group of close friends? Peter, am I your best friend?* We know that Jesus said we are to love him so much that our love for friends and family pales in comparison (Matthew 10 v 37).

This would clearly fit with Jesus' teaching on the way we are to prioritize our affection.

> [28] *One of the teachers of the law ... asked [Jesus], "Of all the commandments, which is the most important?"*
>
> [29] *"The most important one," answered Jesus, "is this: 'Hear, O Israel: The Lord our God, the Lord is one.* [30] *Love the Lord your God with all your heart and with all your soul and with all your mind and with all your strength.'* [31] *The second is this: 'Love your neighbor as yourself.' There is no commandment greater than these."*
>
> (Mark 12 v 28-31)

We are to love God first. The *second* greatest command, Jesus explained, is to love our neighbors—to love others—as we love ourselves.

We all naturally love ourselves. We care for and provide for ourselves. We clothe and feed ourselves. It's loving God and loving others that can be painfully difficult. This kind of love pulls us out of ourselves, turns our focus away from our needs, and directs us beyond our own desires. That's a painful process. It's often referred to as "dying to ourselves." In Romans, the apostle Paul calls it being a "living sacrifice" (Romans 12 v 1-2). And being a sacrifice *hurts*.

This view gives us another powerful application we should seriously consider. We all need to think about how we prioritize our relationship with Jesus. Do we place Jesus above all earthly relationships? Does he even make it onto our short list? If you have to disappoint someone, would Jesus be the top person you would do anything to avoid disappointing? Maybe, as you read these words, Jesus is calling you to make him first in your life today.

OPTION THREE: PETER'S PRIDE

The third option—the one I find the most compelling— is that Jesus is linking back to the last conversation he had with Peter before the crucifixion. That was at a meal too. In that conversation Peter displayed an arrogant kind of love. He was being a bit of a spiritual show-off.

The Bible says that pride comes before a fall (Proverbs 16 v 18). I think pride preceded Peter's fall. And we see it in how Peter responded when Jesus told him he would disown Jesus three times:

²⁷ "You will all fall away," Jesus told them, "for it is written:

> *"'I will strike the shepherd,*
>   *and the sheep will be scattered.'*

²⁸ But after I have risen, I will go ahead of you into Galilee."

²⁹ Peter declared, "Even if all fall away, I will not."

³⁰ "Truly I tell you," Jesus answered, "today—yes, tonight—before the rooster crows twice you yourself will disown me three times."

³¹ But Peter insisted emphatically, "Even if I have to die with you, I will never disown you." And all the others said the same. (Mark 14 v 27-31)

I imagine it was with a catch in the throat that Jesus told the disciples they would all disown him.

After they finished the Passover meal, they sang a hymn and then Jesus explained, "You will all fall away ... for it is written: 'I will strike the shepherd, and the *sheep* will be scattered'" (Mark 14 v 27). But Peter refused to be lumped in with the rest of the *sheep*. He insisted he was different... he was better than that.

At just the worst moment, Peter displayed his horrible social skills and his spiritual problem with pride. He stepped up to the plate and proudly declared, "Even if all fall away, I will not" (Mark 14 v 29). It's as if Peter was saying, *Look Jesus, I have a greater love for you than these fellas do. They might back out but not me!*

That's when Jesus explained to Peter that he would deny Jesus three times that night.

> *"Truly I tell you," Jesus answered, "today—yes, tonight—before the rooster crows twice you yourself will disown me three times." But Peter **insisted emphatically**, "Even if I have to die with you, I will never disown you." And all the others said the same.*
> (Mark 14 v 30-31)

Peter became emphatic. He insisted that he would be true, even if the others weren't. I imagine he raised his voice. Maybe he punched his fist in the air or pounded it against his chest.

While the other disciples joined in at the end, declaring that they would follow Jesus to the death too, I think Peter's bravado sheds light on Jesus' question in John 21. After all that had happened, did Peter still feel as if he loved Jesus more than these other disciples did? Did he still see himself as superior?

GETTING THE POINT

If Jesus was talking about loving fishing, it would make sense for Peter to respond, *Yes, Jesus, I love you more than fishing.* If Jesus was talking about loving the other disciples, it would make sense for Peter to answer, *Yes, Jesus, I love you more than I love the disciples.*

But if Jesus is getting at Peter's pride and his arrogance by asking, "Do you love me more than these?" I think it would make sense for Peter to simply reply, "Yes, Lord, you know that I love you."

Whatever we think Jesus meant by *more than these*, one thing seems clear: Peter got the point. Jesus only used that expression once. The next two times he simply asks Peter if he loves him. Jesus doesn't say, *"more than these."*

Peter's failure to stand firm for Jesus humbled him. Failure humbles us all. Humility is where all learning really begins. What will it take for you to start learning the lessons God wants to teach you? You might pause for a moment and think about that before you keep reading.

A HUMBLE SPIRIT

Jesus wanted Peter to love him, for certain, but he didn't want him to be a religious prig. He didn't want him to be a spiritual show-off. He wanted Peter to have a humble spirit and a simple devotion.

That's what Jesus wants from us too.

This reminds me of a comment I remember my mom using to describe people who were being judgmental. "They're acting like someone who just quit smoking," she would say. What she meant was that people who have just kicked a bad habit can turn around and make the most boastful and obnoxious comments about others who are still struggling.

This can probably be true of people who've just begun a diet, or a person who has just started working out, or, dare I say, someone who has recently given up meat to become a vegetarian.

It can be so easy to look at other people, puff out our chests, and feel as if we're better than them. There's always someone who is doing worse than us, isn't there? But deep down, if we're honest, we know we're no better.

That's because, to a certain extent, we know our own hearts. And God knows us far better than we know ourselves. It's not a pretty picture. But God loves us still. That's the glorious reality of the gospel. *God knows us completely and yet loves us deeply* (Romans 5 v 8).

I like what C.S. Lewis once said: "Don't judge a man by where he is, because you don't know how far he has come." It can be easy to make ourselves look big by making others look small. But God does the opposite. In Jesus, he became small—he became a baby—so that we might know how big God's love really is (Philippians 2 v 5-8).

Christians have been forgiven of much and so should instinctively serve others with humility, particularly those who are struggling and are in the greatest need of our care and support. As Paul says, "Brothers and sisters, if someone is caught in a sin, you who live by the Spirit should restore that person gently. But watch yourselves, or you also may be tempted" (Galatians 6 v 1).

We are all limping on this path together, aren't we? Even in helping others, we are prone to be tempted. We need to gently offer the same help to others that we have received. But too often we take our second of success and look down our noses at those who aren't doing as well.

PROUD TO BE HUMBLE?

Do you struggle with pride? I know I do. We may look at our achievements and successes and allow them to define us. It may even be spiritual pride, as Peter showed here. Or we think about how humble we are and get proud about that!

In my experience, writing a book can be a real test of pride. When it's going well, the temptation is to puff myself up as "the next great author." But when writing is a struggle, I easily see myself as a failure who's unable to do anything at all! Both are problems caused by pride. The reality for each of us is that the gifts we have come *from* the Lord to be used *for* the Lord. Any glory is his alone.

Think about any areas where you might be hanging back from being "all-in" for Jesus because you don't think you need him ("I'm great" pride)—or because you fear that you're too far gone to be any use for Jesus ("If I can't do it, Jesus can't do it" pride).

When Jesus confronts Peter about his pride, we discover two things. First, there is no room for boasting among Jesus' followers. None of us are called to follow him because of our own merits or track record. Second—and wonderfully—this is a reminder that everyone and anyone can come to Jesus and get in on his mission.

The beauty of the gospel is that no one deserves to get in on what Jesus offers. That means no one is too far gone to be used by God. But our pride can get in the way. So God's going to have to rip it away from us before he can really use us. Scripture tells us that God humbles the proud but exalts the humble (Matthew 23 v 12). In other words, God's going to humble us one way or another. We can either get in on it or get run over by it. It's coming either way.

PRIDE IS A BIG DEAL IN THE BIBLE

Even at the Passover meal, Jesus had to deal with the disciples' egos. While Jesus was describing the betrayal and anguish he was about to face, the disciples began arguing about who was going to be the greatest in God's kingdom:

> *A dispute also arose among them as to which of them*
> *was considered to be greatest. Jesus said to them,*
> *The kings of the Gentiles lord it over them; and those*
> *who exercise authority over them call themselves*
> *Benefactors. But you are not to be like that. Instead,*
> *the greatest among you should be like the youngest,*
> *and the one who rules like the one who serves. For who*
> *is greater, the one who is at the table or the one who*
> *serves? Is it not the one who is at the table? But I am*
> *among you as one who serves.*   *(Luke 22 v 24-27)*

Can you believe this? Jesus had just poured his heart out to them about how he was going to suffer and die. And all these guys could do was bicker over who would be greatest?

Which disciples were arguing at the meal? We can't be sure. The Gospel accounts don't tell us which ones. They just say that a dispute arose among them. We can probably safely assume it was all of the disciples.

What we do know for certain is that the very next words out of Jesus's mouth are directed to Peter (who is sometimes also called Simon).

> *"Simon, Simon," Jesus said to Peter, "Satan has asked to sift all of you as wheat. But I have prayed for you, Simon, that your faith may not fail." (Luke 22 v 31-32)*

Immediately after this statement, Jesus warns Peter of his denial. That's the context. Jesus says he's going to die. The disciples argue about who is the greatest. Jesus tells Peter he will deny him three times. Then Peter declares his superior devotion. What a hot mess!

Peter was blinded by his pride. That's what pride does. It makes our faults look like strengths. It leads us to argue. It leads us to jockey for position.

Pride makes us examine the faults of others as if through binoculars, seeing them big with great detail but from a distance. Pride then reverses the binoculars before pointing them at ourselves so that we see our own faults from up close, and as small as possible. As a result, we always look as if we are doing better than everyone around us.

EATING, LOVING, SERVING

We magnify ourselves to minimize others. But Jesus, the Son of God, became small so that we could understand the grandeur of God's love. And the Bible calls us to follow in Jesus' footsteps. We are, in humility, to consider others as better than ourselves (Philippians 2 v 3). That's exactly what we see Jesus doing at this meal:

> *Jesus knew that the Father had put all things under his power, and that he had come from God and was returning to God; so he got up from the meal, took off his outer clothing, and wrapped a towel around his waist. After that, he poured water into a basin and began to wash his disciples' feet, drying them with the towel that was wrapped around him.* (John 13 v 3-5)

This is crazy, isn't it? The eternal Word, Jesus, came to earth as a human (John 1), lived a perfect life (Hebrews 4 v 15), and now knelt washing dust from between the disciples' toes (John 13). This is the model of leadership Jesus was teaching his disciples. This is at the heart of what I think Jesus was communicating to Peter. This is a picture of what God wants from *us*.

I have a small statue in my office that my mom gave me at my seminary graduation. It's of this scene of Jesus washing Peter's feet. Sometimes I'll glance over at it while I'm working and feel the sting of conviction. Too much of what I do has less to do with helping others and more to do with helping myself. God forgive me.

I think it's safe to say that Peter learned the lesson. As an aged man, and an old preacher, he encouraged others to serve with humility. "All of you, clothe yourselves with humility toward one another," Peter wrote, "because, 'God opposes the proud but shows favor to the humble.' Humble yourselves, therefore, under God's mighty hand, that he may lift you up in due time" (1 Peter 5 v 5-6).

Peter's initial problem with pride was clear from his boastful claim that he would never desert Jesus. But by the time he wrote 1 Peter he had learned the value of humility. Between these two points, Jesus had done much work in Peter's heart.

Is there a pride problem in your heart? One way to diagnose that is to think about whether you're willing to help others in ways that aren't fun, that you wouldn't choose to do naturally, and that don't get you praise from others.

SERVANT-HEARTED

I think Peter got the point. The question is, do we? You see, Jesus wants us to love him. But he doesn't want us to be a bunch of religious jerks. He doesn't want us to take the best seats at the table with the assumption that we are better than everyone else.

He wants us to share in his meal. But he wants us to do it as servants.

A mentor of mine used to often say, "You're never more like Jesus than when you serve others." He was so right. But really, isn't there some merit, some virtue, in declaring our superior love for God, so that God and everyone else can know where we stand?

Nope.

A simple "I love you, Jesus" will do. But then we need to pick up a towel and start washing feet. That's the Jesus way. May it be our way too.

3. SERVICE WITH A SMILE

Again Jesus said, "Simon son of John, do you love me?"
He answered, "Yes, Lord, you know that I love you."
Jesus said, "Take care of my sheep."
(John 21 v 16)

Show me how much you love God's people and I will show you how much you love God. You can't get around it. If you're to grow in your love for him, you must grow in your love for them.

God doesn't give us the option of choosing between our love for him and our love for his people. That's because there's a direct connection between how much we love other Christians and how much we love Christ. We can't separate the two.

While it's possible to love people without loving God, it's not possible to love God without loving people. If you love him, you will begin to care for the things he cares about. It might start small at first. But it will grow.

Trust me. It will grow. It must.

A bigger heart toward God will mean a bigger heart toward others. We will either get both or we will get neither. If we love him more, we will begin to love them more. If we refuse to love them more we will stifle our love for God. We aren't given a choice between the two but a command to do both.

IN SEARCH OF DRAGONS

Let me explain this by personalizing a sermon illustration I heard years ago. One time my son Isaiah lost a toy dragon at a local park. Later that evening he was really upset. So, I did what any loving father would do. I told him I'd dip into his college fund and buy him a new one. Then I promptly sent him back to bed.

Just kidding. I'm too cheap to do anything like that. Let me rephrase: I did what any thoughtful (and cheap) dad would do. I grabbed a flashlight and headed for the park.

I searched high and low for this silly plastic dragon. I didn't do it because I loved the toy. I didn't love the toy. I loved the boy. I searched for the toy because I love the boy who loves the toy.

This only partly illustrates the point, of course, as I never did love the toy. But the truth is, if we learn to love God, we will also learn to love the things he loves. It may take time, but it will happen. Along the way we may discover ourselves doing things—serving people—not entirely because we love them, but because we love *him*. Our love for him will demand our love for them:

> *Dear friends, since God so loved us, we also ought to love one another. No one has ever seen God; but if we love one another, God lives in us and his love is made complete in us.* (1 John 4 v 11-12)

We see this in Jesus' conversation with Peter. Jesus asks Peter three times if he loves him. Peter answers yes each time. But every time Jesus comes back with a specific command. Did you notice that?

- v 15: Feed my lambs.

- v 16: Take care of my sheep.

- v 17: Feed my sheep.

Every time that Peter says, "I love you," Jesus tells him to feed the sheep. His question about Peter's love is directly tied to his command to care for the sheep. But why can't Peter just love Jesus and leave the sheep out of it?

We may feel that way sometimes too. *"Why do I need the church?"* we might wonder. *"Why can't I just love God but leave church out of it?"*

Why not? Because you can't separate loving Jesus from loving Jesus' sheep. You can't split up the shepherd from the sheep. They're a package deal.

DUMPY, WOBBLY, AND NEEDY

Sheep are a common picture of God's people in Scripture. If we got to pick which animal the Bible uses to describe us, I'm sure we would've come up with something more exciting than sheep. Sheep aren't brave like lions, strong like elephants, or busy like beavers. They're dumpy, wobbly, and needy.

Yep, that's us. Nailed it! We're a bunch of sheep, aren't we? We may try to hide it, even from ourselves, but underneath we're a bunch of dumpy, wobbly, needy sheep.

How could God ever love *us*? Well, the same way the Bible tells us to love other stinky sheep. We don't love them because they're perfect. We love them because *God's love is perfect*.

As the Bible explains, we love God "because he first loved us" (1 John 4 v 19). We love others for the same reason: God loved them first. And the more his love works in us, and the more it grows in us, the more it will eventually work through us and out to others.

And let's remember that love in the Bible isn't all flowers and chocolates. It's messy. It's painful. It's risky. Jesus' love for his sheep led to hardship and persecution, and ultimately to death. Our love for others will be costly too.

Look back at Jesus' conversation with Peter. Jesus didn't tell Peter to love the sheep. He told him to *feed* the sheep: to take care of them. The love should follow. But even if it doesn't follow right away, the command still remains.

At the heart of this conversation between Jesus and Peter is love for God and love for others. Jesus said these two loves summarize the entire Old Testament (Matthew 22 v 36-40). All of the Hebrew Scriptures can be expressed in one four-letter word: *love*.

In other words, if we miss this—if we miss the priority of loving God and loving others—then we miss the whole show. We can't pick and choose. We can't commit to loving God but refuse to love his people. These two great commands are forever wed together. And what God has joined together, let no one separate.

I HATE YOUR BODY!

This reminds me of a couple examples that my Bible teacher, Dr. Russell Moore, uses to explain the church. Imagine if someone came up to you and said, "I just want you to know that I think you're great. I love you. It's your body I hate." Would you consider that a compliment? No. You might want to punch them in the face.

If someone came up to me and said, "Dan, I want you to know I think you're great. Your sermons and your books are really helpful. I love you, really. It's your wife I hate." That wouldn't be a compliment at all. I might want to punch them in the face.

Okay, this is starting to get violent. Hopefully you get the point.

Both of these examples are straight out of Scripture. Both a *body* (Colossians 1 v 24) and a *bride* (Revelation

21 v 9) are ways of describing the church in the New Testament. My teacher's point was plain enough. If we love Jesus, we will love Jesus' body. If we love Christ, we will love his bride. If we love God, we will love the church.

So, show me how much you love the church, and I'll show you how much you love Christ.

At this point, you might want to tell me how imperfect your church is. You might argue that it's filled with hypocrites—with people who don't perfectly live out what they say they believe. Do you see where I'm heading with this?

Are *you* perfect? Do you ever fail to live out what you say you believe? Does God still love you? Well, then, let's extend that love to others. You and I don't deserve God's love any more than they do, and they don't need it any less than we do.

Seriously, do we think we're doing God a favor when we say we love him but live in a way that says, "I hate your body. I hate your bride." And we can't just love the idea of the church. The church isn't just an idea—it's real people who gather in Jesus' name. So we have to love real people in a real church.

FIND A FLOCK

We can't just love the idea of sheep. We are to love *real* sheep. But sheep smell, don't they? Yeah, so do we. So do you.

What are you going to do about it? Live in isolation? You can't be all that God has created you to be by yourself—too much of the Christian life centers on what the Bible calls "one another."

There are around fifty different "one another" references in the New Testament: accept one another (Romans 15 v 7), teach one another (Colossians 3 v 16), care for one another (Galatians 6 v 2), forgive one another (Ephesians 4 v 32), offer hospitality to one another (1 Peter 4 v 9), and meet with one another (Hebrews 10 v 25), just to name a few. We aren't meant to do the Christian life alone. We're meant to do it with one another.

A friend of mine used to say that you can't love *the* church until you love *a* church. What he meant is that we can't just love the idea of the church in the broad sense of all believers, all followers of Jesus. We have to translate that love to a specific group of people, a local church, a community of faith, to whom we commit ourselves.

That means that your love for the church should have faces associated with it: real people you know—people with whom you've laughed, cried, mourned, rejoiced, played, worked, and shared meals. And while, biblically, the church is not a building, your love for the church should have some physical address associated with it: a place where you gather with other followers of Jesus to fulfill all of the "one anothers" of Scripture.

THE THREE T'S

Trust me, we're going to need each other. Life is tough. It's a hard world and we're fragile beings. We need community. That's why the apostle Paul tells us that we're to be devoted to one another (Romans 12 v 10).

A helpful way I've heard for thinking about our devotion to one another is with three T's: our *time*, our *talents*, and our *treasure*. Life circumstances beyond our control may limit our participation in any or all of these categories. But these three T's provide a helpful way to consider our contribution and commitment to other Christians.

The "one another" commands are far more than just a code of conduct for Sunday mornings. And while our devotion to one another might begin within the context of a weekly worship service, it certainly shouldn't end there. The needs of any particular Christian community will reach far beyond the walls of a church building.

Your *time* is your presence with other Christians. It's your commitment to meet with other believers, as much as you're able, for mutual encouragement. It's doing life with one another; it's sharing meals together; it's supporting one another. Sometimes it's answering your phone at 3 am when you're the only person someone can think of to call. God has given you time to invest in others.

Your *talents* are your gifts and passions. You might express these gifts and passions through service projects, leading a Bible study, visiting the elderly, mentoring a teenager, or serving in any number of ministries at your church. Just know this: in your church family there will be people with needs that are peculiarly shaped in the form of *your* talents. God has uniquely gifted you to serve them, to help meet their practical and spiritual needs.

You have resources that are useful for meeting the needs of others and supporting the work of your church. And I'm not just talking about money. By *treasure*, I mean the things God has blessed you with to meet needs— your own and those of others. For example, if you have a pick-up truck, you have a resource that can be really useful for others (all the truck people know exactly what I'm talking about). God has blessed you with resources so that you can be a blessing to others.

How you use your time, talents, and treasure in the church is an expression of your devotion to one another. So, how are you doing with the three T's? You might write out time, talents, and treasure on a piece of paper and jot out a few goals for each: ways you'd like to grow in expressing your commitment to God's people.

SOME OBSTACLES TO ONE ANOTHER

God's love, like God's blessings, is never intended to be a one-way street or a dead end. God didn't create you to be a cul-de-sac. He made you to be like a well-traveled highway where his love for you and your love for him are highly accessible, touching the lives of as many people as possible. That's why loving others is critical in becoming who God wants you to be.

Our brokenness will make this difficult at times. Sin will make us want to hide from others. Sins like lust and anger will draw us further into ourselves instead of pushing us outward toward others. But love for God will continue to push us beyond our comfort zones and away from our hiding places.

None of these things come easily. None of it is painless. Nothing worth fighting for ever is.

Sins like gossip, slander, and envy will make us see others as objects or competition. Sins like bitterness and an unwillingness to forgive will be like gigantic stone walls separating us. These walls are going to have to come down.

There are also numerous other challenges that will make the "one another" aspects of the Christian life hard and even, at times, nearly impossible. And they're not all necessarily sinful. Anxiety, depression, job requirements, and family needs can all keep people from regular worship at times, even when they sincerely want to participate.

Still, the Bible shows us that it's in the community of those who follow Jesus—in the church—where we can learn to carry one another's burdens (Galatians 6 v 2). And a part of a loving community should be support for those whose struggles make participation tough. We must believe God's love is strong enough to break through these walls we build and big enough to begin healing our brokenness.

THE SHEPHERD AND THE SHEEP

The Bible describes God as the good shepherd who sticks with us through the good times and the bad, provides for us in the presence of our enemies, and leads us through danger with the promise to guide us safely home (Psalm 23). And in the Gospels, Jesus describes himself as the good shepherd who lays down his life for his sheep (John 10 v 11).

So, it's not so bad being called sheep if that means we get a shepherd like Jesus, is it?

And, as the good shepherd, Jesus closely identifies with his sheep. If someone messes with the sheep, they are really messing with the shepherd. Saul (later Paul), the New Testament rebel-turned-apostle, learned this the hard way. He was on his way to persecute Christians when Jesus confronted him. Here's the encounter:

> [1] *Meanwhile, Saul was still breathing out murderous threats against the Lord's disciples. He went to the high priest* [2] *and asked him for letters to the synagogues in Damascus, so that if he found any there who belonged to the Way, whether men or women, he might take them as prisoners to Jerusalem.* [3] *As he neared Damascus on his journey, suddenly a light from heaven flashed around him.* [4] *He fell to the ground and heard a voice say to him, "Saul, Saul, why do you persecute me?"* [5] *"Who are you, Lord?" Saul asked. "I am Jesus, whom you are persecuting," he replied.* (Acts 9 v 1-5)

Did you notice that? Who did Jesus say Saul was persecuting? Jesus had already returned to heaven before Saul came onto the stage. As far as we know, Jesus and Saul never met prior to Jesus ascending into heaven. This was their first meeting.

Saul hadn't been persecuting Jesus. He had been persecuting Christians, followers of "the Way" (v 2). So, why would Jesus tell Saul he was persecuting him?

That's because Jesus takes it personally when someone messes with his sheep. He so closely identifies with his people that when you mess with them, you are really messing with him. If you reject them, you are rejecting him. If you serve them, you are serving him.

That why Jesus said that if we give even a cup of cold water in his name, we are really giving it to him (Matthew 10 v 42). When we clothe the poor and feed the hungry, we are told that we are really serving Jesus (Matthew 25 v 37-40). That's how closely Jesus identifies with his people. Our service to them is service to him.

You can't separate the shepherd from the sheep. But we try to do that all the time, don't we? We want the love and protection of the shepherd, but we don't want to be bothered by other sheep. If one sheep gets lost, we'd rather have the shepherd stick with us than go looking for them (Luke 15). We're going to need God's help to create in us a love for others.

Is that something you struggle with? Have you been reading this chapter thinking it's just not for you? If so, now would be a good time to stop for a moment; think about what it is that makes it hard for you to love and serve other Christians; then turn those thoughts into prayer. If you ask God to grow your heart so that it becomes more like Christ's heart for his flock, he will.

GOD'S LABORATORY

If you were to have breakfast with Jesus this morning, I bet he'd deal with you in a similar way that he did with Peter. He would start by asking about your heart.

Imagine sitting in the presence of the one who died for you. How would that feel? You might want to say, "I love you, Jesus," but maybe it would be hard to get the words out.

Our love is so feeble in comparison to his, isn't it? And yet his question, "Do you love me?" requires an answer. "Yes" we might cough out between sobs of gratitude. "I love... I want to love you... Lord."

"Then feed my sheep," Jesus would likely respond.

So, show me how much you love the sheep, and I'll show you how much you love the shepherd. It's a package deal. Of course, it's easy to love the shepherd. He's Jesus. Jesus is perfect.

Sheep, on the other hand, aren't. They're far from perfect. And they're much more difficult to love. That's because a lot of times the sheep don't—*we* don't—look all that much like the shepherd. But since Jesus is the good shepherd, not only will he lead us home; he's also going to lead us to love the other sheep along the way.

If you're not at all connected to a church, that would be a good place to begin. Ask a Christian friend you respect what church family they belong to. To grow as a follower of Jesus, to obey the "one another" passages of Scripture, it's vitally important to plug into a church that believes and teaches the Bible. Don't let another week pass without making every reasonable effort to worship, learn, and grow with other followers of Jesus.

Maybe you already have a church, but you're finding it difficult to really engage. I understand. It can be hard to trust others. It can be difficult to be vulnerable, especially if you've been hurt in the past. But God will give you opportunities to use your time, talents, and treasure to glorify him and bless others if you look for them and if you're willing to take advantage of them. Are you?

You need to keep in mind that the church is a messy place. But it exists for messy people like you and me. We will let each other down. But this messy place is God's laboratory for cultivating your Christian character. So, find a church you can commit to as if your spiritual growth depends upon it. Because it does.

You need community. You may be tempted to think you're strong enough to do it alone, but remember the

Bible says that pride comes before a fall. That's what happened to Peter. And when Jesus forgave Peter, the first command he gave him was to care for the sheep.

That's because you can't be obedient to Jesus without loving *the* church—without loving *a* church.

We're just a bunch of dumpy, wobbly, needy sheep. But we have a good shepherd. And he made us to love him and to love each other. It's God's design. It's the aim of the entire Bible. It's written into the blueprints of the universe.

4. A SIDE OF BACON

Then he said to him, "Follow me!"
(John 21 v 19)

Some stories are told again and again because they really pack a punch. Like the one about the chicken and the pig. These two tasty farmyard animals contribute to breakfast buffets around the world every day, but in very different ways.

When you have eggs and bacon for breakfast you can be certain of two things: the chicken made an *investment*; the pig made a *sacrifice*. The chicken laid an egg and went on with life. For the pig, it was the end of the road.

When it comes to the Christian life, we're much more willing to be the chicken than the pig, aren't we? We're willing to give a little—maybe even quite a lot—but don't ask us to give all.

But what if God is calling us to more than just making an investment? What if God is calling us to do more than

DAN DEWITT

lay an egg? What if he wants us to be like the pig? *Are you chicken?*

TWO WORDS THAT WILL CHANGE YOUR LIFE

This is where the breakfast conversation between Jesus and Peter takes a far more serious tone. Jesus drops a bomb in the middle of their morning dialogue.

Jesus goes from talking about loving sheep to telling Peter he's going to lose his life. I imagine this was a difficult conversation. But Jesus does it with style. He's straight to the point. *Peter, if you love me, you will feed my sheep. And then you're gonna die.* Full stop.

If I were Jesus, I'd be like, "Bro, sit down. Prepare yourself. You know that I love you, right? You know that I gave my life for you, right? You know that heaven is going to be awesome, right?" And then, and only then, would I break the news to him as softly as possible.

Yeah, that's not how Jesus did it:

"Very truly I tell you, when you were younger you dressed yourself and went where you wanted; but when you are old you will stretch out your hands, and someone else will dress you and lead you where you do not want to go." Jesus said this to indicate the kind of death by which Peter would glorify God. Then he said to him, "Follow me!" (John 21 v 18-19)

Jesus just drops this and lets it marinate for a moment. There's no soft delivery. There's no gentle follow-up.

There's no rosy let-down.

He doesn't say, *Peter, now that I've told you this, remember I will love you for all of eternity. I'll never leave you. And I'll be standing at heaven's gate waiting to receive you.*

Nope. Jesus tells Peter he is going to die and then offers him two simple words: "Follow me." These two words, these three syllables, can gloriously wreck our lives.

PIGS OR CHICKENS?

Jesus says, "Follow me" to all of us without exception, qualification, or apology. Jesus wants pigs, not chickens. We'd rather lay an egg, wouldn't we? We'd prefer to leave the bacon bit to someone else. But Jesus calls us, like Peter, to follow him no matter what the cost.

The cost for Peter was going to be very high indeed. And as we'll see, he doesn't take it well. Would you?

When you first read this passage, it's not entirely clear what Jesus is talking about. Jesus tells Peter that people will take him when he's old and make him wear something he doesn't want to wear and go somewhere he doesn't want to go. Sounds like a bizarre elderly kidnapping fashion-show kind of thing to me. But John, *the disciple whom Jesus loved*, clears this up for us.

John explains, "Jesus said this to indicate the kind of death by which Peter would glorify God" (John 21 v 19). John's short disclaimer, *FYI, Peter's gonna die!* doesn't really soften things too much. We'll have more to say about John in a moment. For now, just know that John is more than a mere narrator in this passage. He plays a pretty big role in Peter's response.

THE DECISION THAT DEFINES YOU

For Peter, this was the heart of his commitment to Jesus, the point of decision. His love for Jesus would cost him his life. Was he willing to pay the cost? Are we? Will we heed these two words that call us to offer up everything, to put it all on the table, to hold nothing back?

You see, this isn't a decision we can postpone until something big comes up. This is the kind of commitment that we have to make in advance. Peter made this decision over breakfast by the sea. Where will you be when you make the decision to follow Jesus wherever he leads, no matter what the consequences or costs are?

You might say that you made that decision a long time ago. But you know as well as I do that every day brings new circumstances that test our willingness to obey. In what way is Jesus calling you to follow him today? Or maybe, turn that on its head and ask yourself: in what ways are you choosing to ignore him and do your own thing right now?

For Peter, there was no immediate threat. There were no soldiers waiting to take him away. There was just the smoke from a campfire, roasted fish, and the sound of those two piercing words: "Follow me."

It's the decisions we make in easy times that prepare us for the hard times. That's why, at this very moment, by God's grace, you could stop trying to be the boss of your own life and submit to Jesus. You can decide to follow.

For some readers, this might be the first time in a long time that you've wanted to make that all-in kind of decision, rather than being half-in or half-out. Or it could be the very first time you've decided to follow Jesus. (If so, that's wonderful—why not grab the moment right now? Just talk very naturally to Jesus. Tell him you know you've failed him in the past, but that you want to follow him from now on. Ask him to help you. He will.) For others, it might seem like the millionth time. That's because following Jesus is a daily commitment. We can never mark it off our to-do list.

To be clear, from heaven's perspective there's a moment when we pass over from death to life (John 5 v 24). The word we often use in the church to describe this decisive event is *conversion*. Though you might not remember the specific date or time when this happened to you, if you are a Christian, you know that indeed it did happen.

So, while becoming a Christian happens at a point in your life, the journey of following Christ is marked by daily decisions. This is what the Christian life looks like. It's the daily grind of obedience.

And since none of us obey perfectly, we are always wrestling with those two words Jesus said to Peter. We have to come back to them again and again. We never outgrow them. Christians never graduate from daily following Christ.

Now, obviously, most of us won't die as martyrs like Peter. So, the real question is, for you and me, are we willing to live sacrificially? We might not be killed for our faith, but we can die to our sinful choices and our selfish ambitions. It can start today. It can begin right now, before you turn the next page.

I could give a list of sins or attitudes that could be keeping you from following Jesus today. But my bet is that I don't have to guess your struggle for you to know what it is. Probably the first thing that comes to mind when you contemplate the question of "What is keeping me from following Jesus today?" is the very thing about which God wants to deal with you right now. Will you let him?

I'd encourage you to take a moment right now and consider those things that come to mind. Would you be willing to find a Christian friend you trust and share with them? Together you can pray for God to give you strength to do what you need to do to obey Jesus' invitation to follow him. This really is a fork in the road. How you respond will play an important role in your future growth.

CROSS-SHAPED OBEDIENCE

We can be certain of this: if we decide to follow Jesus, it won't be easy or come cheap. Nothing of value ever does.

But the alternative—choosing to disobey Jesus—will cost you more in the long run. So choose wisely.

Here's the picture Jesus painted of what it looks like to follow him.

> *Whoever wants to be my disciple must deny themselves and take up their cross daily and follow me. For whoever wants to save their life will lose it, but whoever loses their life for me will save it. What good is it for someone to gain the whole world, and yet lose or forfeit their very self?* (Luke 9 v 23-25)

The cross is a picture of death. In Jesus' time you wouldn't hang a cross on your wall for decoration or around your neck as a piece of jewelry. That would be the modern-day equivalent of framing a picture of an electric chair and placing it next to your dinner table. It wouldn't make any sense.

When Jesus struggled beneath the heavy burden of a large wooden beam draped over his whip-savaged shoulders, it was the ultimate act of obedience. Earlier, in the Garden of Gethsemane, Jesus had asked his Father if there were any way other than the cross. As drops of sweat like blood fell from Jesus' face, he prayed, "... yet not my will, but yours be done" (Luke 22 v 42). For Jesus, obedience to the Father meant carrying his cross.

Our cross comes to us in the shape of obedience as well. It comes as those two words, "Follow me." There are probably a million reasons we could come up with to postpone or ignore this call to follow. Fear, doubt, and sin are a few common ones. But the one who calls us to carry a cross for him is the one who carried a cross for us. That should be the only reason we need to follow him.

Jesus carried his cross to the top of a small hill outside Jerusalem, where he died for our sins so that we could have forgiveness. And his two-word invitation bids us follow in his steps. Yes, following Jesus is a death march.

Does that sound like an exaggeration to you? While it's true that it's dangerous to be a Christian in many parts of today's world, most of us in the West don't face risk to life and limb. But it was Jesus himself who described following him as carrying our cross, so we must take seriously the risk which that's going to cause to our daily patterns of living. He calls us to die to sin and self.

WATCH OUT FOR POTHOLES

Love for Jesus leads us down a certain kind of path. We won't follow perfectly every step of the way, that's for certain. But Jesus will lead us down a path of obedience. To follow him will demand that we surrender daily.

The path may be filled with potholes and self-inflicted detours. But if we are to follow him, we have to begin by saying yes. We have to call him boss. We have to submit to him as Lord.

This is hard. In fact, it's impossible without God's help. But for all who desire this, who want to live this way, who want to follow Jesus, God will give both the desire and the ability to do it (Philippians 2 v 13). God will accomplish this for us, in us, and through us.

God will do it. But it will come with a cost. It will kill us. But something beautiful can grow out of the soil of our surrender.

This reminds me of one of the apostle Paul's longest letters. He spends eleven chapters out of sixteen in Romans unpacking deep truths about who God is and what he has done for us in Christ. Then chapter 12 begins with a punchy application of what our personal response should be to the grace of God:

"Therefore," Paul writes, "I urge you, brothers and sisters, in view of God's mercy, to offer your bodies as a living sacrifice, holy and pleasing to God—this is your true and proper worship" (Romans 12 v 1). This is where love for God, and gratitude for his mercy, leads us. It leads us to submission. It leads to living sacrifices.

Being a sacrifice isn't for chickens. Jesus doesn't water it down. He says it will look like a cross. It will look like death. And Jesus wraps the whole thing up in those two little words: follow me.

Of course, Peter's life wasn't just about dying. Between breakfast on the beach and his death by execution, Peter lived a life full of opportunity, joy, and service. He preached to thousands. He travelled. He told both the powerful and the poor about Christ. At one point he even got rescued by an angel! (Acts 2 v 14, 40-41; 10 v 1-48; 12 v 1-17) Jesus used Peter to change the world. He can use you too.

In other words, what Peter was being called to die for is also the greatest thing to live for. Who knows what Jesus is calling us to do and be, as we accept the cost and sacrifice of following him? But we can know that, whatever it is, it will be better than a life of hanging back and hanging on to our comforts and compromises.

LOST IN COMPARISON

Peter, of course, is never at a loss for words. His eyes dart away from Jesus to *the disciple whom Jesus loved*. If Peter is anything like me, you can feel his sense of injustice and rage in the words that follow. You can sense his insecurity. You can hear his unbelief.

There's something about John's nickname I didn't notice until reading a devotional by Beth Moore. Only the Gospel of John, written by John, ever calls John "the disciple whom Jesus loved." Matthew, Mark, and Luke don't do it—only John. And in John's Gospel, the only person who ever calls John that is the narrator, who is coincidentally John. If that's how John sees himself, maybe that's one reason why Peter reacts the way he does.

Here's how *the disciple Jesus loved* described the scene:

> *Peter turned and saw that **the disciple whom Jesus loved** was following them. (This was the one who had*

leaned back against Jesus at the supper and had said,
"Lord, who is going to betray you?") When Peter saw him,
he asked, "Lord, what about him?" (John 21 v 20-21)

Forgive me for picking on John. I believe God inspired the Bible so even this detail is a part of God's plan. But the fact that John seems to be the only person who uses his nickname might shed some light on Peter's response.

Peter turns toward the guy who is constantly referring to himself as the disciple whom Jesus loved, likely points his finger at him, looks at Jesus with eyebrows raised, and says in a huff, "What about that guy?"

Jesus' response to Peter is short: "What is that to you?" In other words, that's none of your business. Then Jesus repeats those two life-changing words: "Follow me."

Maybe you can relate. "How can Jesus ask me to do this," you might ask, whatever this is, "when that person over there has it so easy?" How can Jesus ask me to forgive something so wrong? How can Jesus ask me to go somewhere so far? How can Jesus expect me to do something so hard? How can Jesus ask me to pay a price so great?

After all, other people don't have to do that, we think to ourselves.

Yes, but Jesus doesn't ask us to carry someone else's cross, does he? No, he asks us to carry our own cross.

We don't get to choose our crosses. We get to choose whether or not we will obey those two simple words. No,

Jesus doesn't let us pick our cross. He just calls us to pick it up and follow him.

This reminds me of the scene in C.S. Lewis's story *The Horse and His Boy*. A young boy named Shasta is on a long journey. He's hungry, lonely, and scared. Aslan, the Christ-like lion in the Narnia stories, walks beside him and begins a conversation.

Once Shasta learns to trust the lion, he asks about what has happened to one of his good friends. Aslan tells the boy, "I am telling you your story, not hers. I tell no one any story but his own." That is essentially what Jesus told Peter: *I'm not telling you John's story. I'm telling you your story. Follow me.*

We may point our finger at the disciple whom Jesus loves in our lives, raise our eyebrows, and say in a huff to Jesus, "What about them?" But deep down we know the answer. It's none of our business. We're not called to carry their cross anymore than they are called to carry ours. We can encourage and support one another. But we all have to carry our own cross. It's the cost of being a disciple.

Let me ask you, did someone give you this book? If they're a mature Christian, it may help to look at their life as an example of what following Jesus looks like (though I guarantee they won't be doing it perfectly). But be careful not to start comparing unhelpfully. Jesus wants to talk to you about *your* heart, not theirs.

Not only does Jesus prevent us from comparing ourselves with others; he also doesn't give us a ton of details about where he is going to lead us. That's hard for all of us because we want to know what's next. What comes after this first step of obedience? I can do it today, but what about tomorrow? But Jesus gives us a *directive* (follow me), not *directions* (this is precisely where I will lead you).

WHAT'S YOUR NEXT STEP?

Jesus calls us to follow, one step at a time, with no guarantee of where our obedience will take us next or how much it might cost. We want a detailed map. But Jesus just gives us a destination and tells us to trust him every step of the way.

If we take this breakfast conversation in John 21 to heart, it could radically change our lives. Jesus wants us to love him with a servant-like attitude. He wants us to care for his people, the sheep. And he wants us to follow him regardless of the consequences.

Of course, the consequences will look different for all of us. I have a friend who had a really prosperous job, but his firm was involved in what he viewed to be unethical behavior. He took a massive pay cut in order to start over with another company so he could be obedient to Jesus.

Some other friends left the comfort of living near family to move to the other side of the world as missionaries. They've admitted that it can be a temptation to compare themselves with others who don't seem as committed. But Jesus doesn't tell us someone else's story, does he? He only tells us our own. Even if we make what seems to us to be a very great sacrifice, Jesus still doesn't want us to compare.

Just today I read of a young girl named Leah Sharibu, who is paying a large price because of following Jesus. A month ago Muslim insurgents abducted her and over 100 other girls from a school in Nigeria. Most of the girls have since been released. But it's reported that Leah hasn't been released because she refuses to renounce her faith in Christ. Today as I write this, it's her fifteenth birthday.

Following Jesus isn't easy or cheap. It will look different for all of us. Don't be mistaken—it will cost us all something. But so will disobedience. Which will you choose?

Our lives hang in the balance of how we respond to those two simple words: *follow me*.

It's only the epic power of God's grace that can move us out of our ruts, past our comparisons, and on our way of obedience. So, let the adventure begin. Who knows where it may lead? But we can be certain of this: we have a reliable guide who will be with us every single step of the way.

5. CRACKED EGGS

Early in the morning, Jesus stood on the shore, but the disciples did not realize that it was Jesus.
(John 21 v 4)

Peter saw Jesus do some remarkable things. One time, Peter's mother-in-law was deathly ill. Jesus healed her (Mark 1 v 30-31). Another time, Peter almost drowned. Jesus saved him (Matthew 14 v 38-31). Jesus never let Peter down.

Jesus saw Peter do some remarkably stupid things. One time, Peter told Jesus not to go to the cross. Jesus told him, "Get behind me, Satan" (Mark 8 v 33). Another time, Peter attacked someone with a sword to try to keep Jesus from going to the cross. Jesus told him, "No more of this!" (John 18 v 10; Luke 22 v 50-51) Peter let Jesus down a lot.

Jesus was a far better friend to Peter than Peter was to Jesus. Can you relate? I know I can. If you ever feel like a failure, the Bible is for you. The gospel is for you. Jesus is for you. This breakfast conversation between Jesus and Peter is for you.

I love how author Bob Goff describes this passage in John's Gospel. He says, "When Jesus rose from the dead he didn't make a speech to the world; he made breakfast for his friends." That pretty well sums it up.

After Peter denied Jesus three times, Jesus made him breakfast on the beach and gave him three opportunities to say, "I love you."

This is powerful grace. This is the kind of forgiveness that can transform a life. After this conversation we don't find Peter fishing again. We just find him preaching. But before we get to the good part of the story, we have to get through the bad part.

PETER'S LAST STAND

Before his execution, Jesus shared his last meal with defectors. In the coming hours, everyone sitting around the table would let him down in one way or another. This had to be one lonely meal. To top things off, Peter was insistent that he would stick with Jesus to the end:

> "Simon, Simon, Satan has asked to sift all of you as wheat. But I have prayed for you, Simon, that your faith may not fail. And when you have turned back, strengthen your brothers." But he replied, "Lord, I am ready to go with you to prison and to death." Jesus

answered, "I tell you, Peter, before the rooster crows
today, you will deny three times that you know me."
(Luke 22 v 31-34)

What strikes me is how gentle Jesus was with the very people who would turn away from him. Even the way he talked to Peter was kind. He didn't seem to be raising his voice or pounding his fist on the table. He was preparing Peter for what was to come.

When they finished the meal, they sang a song and then left for a garden where Jesus prayed. Then all hell broke loose. But even in the face of imminent danger, Jesus demonstrated love and grace to his followers. He was even kind to those who came to take him away.

"If you are looking for me," Jesus told the soldiers coming to arrest him, "then let these men go" (John 18 v 8). Just as Jesus predicted, the disciples would soon leave him to face his trial alone. But first, Peter tried to make good on his word to not disappoint Jesus.

Peter pulled out a sword and thrashed at the high priest's servant, who was a part of the arrest party. It looks as if Peter was going for his face. He ended up cutting off his ear (John 18 v 10).

This was Peter's last ounce of courage. This was Peter's last stand. But even in this act of bravery, Peter got it wrong.

"No more of this!" Jesus told him (Luke 22 v 51). Then Jesus did the unthinkable. He touched the side of the servant's head and healed him. Even when Peter was trying to do something right, Jesus had to clean up after his mess. But this was just the beginning. Things were about to get far worse.

A ROOSTER AT DAWN

The soldiers took Jesus away. Mark's Gospel points out that Peter "followed ... at a distance" (Mark 14 v 54). That implies that Peter was close enough to see what was going on but far enough away to hopefully stay out of trouble. I think we sometimes follow Jesus like that too.

Peter's distance didn't provide adequate cover. A young girl saw him and asked if he was one of Jesus' friends. As he walked by, Peter coolly denied that he knew Jesus (v 66-68).

This reminds me of a scene in C.S. Lewis's space trilogy where a character named Mark is being recruited by a sinister group of scientists. Mark's desire to be a part of the inner ring, the cool group, the ones with the power, leads him to compromise. Lewis describes how Mark crossed over to the dark side without even noticing:

> But the moment of his consent almost escaped his notice; certainly, there was no struggle, no sense of turning a corner. There may have been a time in the world's history when such moments fully revealed their gravity ... But, for him, it all slipped past in a chatter of laughter.
> (That Hideous Strength, p 158)

Peter's slide into dishonesty and cowardice followed a similar pattern. This moment seemed lost upon him. He missed the significance of this first denial. At this point, as Jesus was being dragged to death, Peter wouldn't even admit he knew him. It was dark and the air was cold, so Peter walked over to a fire to keep warm. I wonder if he even realized what had just happened.

Meanwhile, Jesus was being questioned. In typical style, Jesus answered questions with more questions. *Smack!* An official hit Jesus and demanded, "Is this the way you answer the high priest?" (John 18 v 22).

I imagine Peter hearing the sound of the man's hand hitting the side of Jesus' face. I can see Peter's eyebrows rising as his stomach sank. *This is really happening?* he must have thought. *I have to play this cool or they might notice my concern. They might figure out I'm Jesus' friend.*

Whatever was going through Peter's mind, his plan to follow from a distance continued to prove unsuccessful. A man looking at Peter's face illuminated by the fire asked him, "You aren't one of his disciples too, are you?" "I am not," Peter said (John 18 v 25; Luke 22 v 58). Strike two.

You would expect Peter to connect the dots. Jesus had told Peter that he would deny Jesus three times. After the second time, it should have hit him that things were going exactly as Jesus predicted. But fear, anxiety, and adrenaline can play havoc with our logic, can't they?

Peter wasn't thinking straight. He was doing all he could to blend in with these soldiers and to distance himself from Jesus. That's what sin does to us. It makes us irrational. It lures us toward the things that kill us and away from what can give us life.

Then the heat turned up. A relative of the man whose ear Peter had cut off challenged him. "Didn't I see you with him in the garden?" he asked (John 18 v 26). If anyone had been paying attention to Peter in the garden, it would have been the relative of the man with a near-fatal head wound.

At this point, if Peter says yes, not only is he in danger of being affiliated with Jesus; he's also going to face an angry cousin looking to settle the score. Being from an Italian family (on my mom's side), I've learned this much over many pasta dishes throughout the years—you don't mess with family. What was Peter to do?

This was no easy moment. It's difficult situations like these that expose weaknesses in our character—soft spots in our commitment to Jesus. These moments reveal our true selves. They bring us face to face with who we really are. And we might not like what we see.

Mark's Gospel tells us that Peter began to swear: "He began to call down curses, and he swore to them, 'I don't know this man you're talking about'" (Mark 14 v 71). His rage gave way to the crowing of a rooster announcing the dawn (John 18 v 27). But for Peter, it was announcing a whole lot more.

This was a sound Peter had heard thousands of times. But never like this. Luke's Gospel records an interesting detail. By this time Peter was close enough that not only could he see Jesus; Jesus could see him:

> *The Lord turned and looked straight at Peter. Then Peter remembered the word the Lord had spoken to him: "Before the rooster crows today, you will disown me three times."*   *(Luke 22 v 61)*

That look must have cut through Peter's heart. Luke makes that point clearly. After Jesus looked at him, Peter ran out of the courtyard and "wept bitterly" (Luke 22 v 62). And as Peter ran away, the soldiers began beating Jesus.

THE EMPTY TOMB THAT FILLS THE WORLD

The guards blindfolded Jesus and began to punch him. Peter may even have heard the sounds of Jesus groaning in pain as he ran off. "Who hit you?" the soldiers mocked as they took turns (Luke 22 v 64).

There's a story in the Old Testament that reminds me of what the soldiers did next. One time, King David sent a peaceful delegation to another nation. Instead of welcoming David's men, they disgraced them.

They cut the back section off their robes (think medical gowns), and shaved their beards halfway off (2 Samuel 10). When David heard the news, he told them to wait until their beards grew back before coming home. He didn't mention their robes. I'm guessing he assumed they would figure it out.

The soldiers did something very similar to Jesus. But they didn't just cut part of his robe off. They stripped him naked (Matthew 27 v 33-36). And they didn't shave off half his beard. They pulled it out by the handful (Isaiah 50 v 6). Then they nailed him to a cross and hoisted it high in the air. And after about six hours of hanging there, Jesus died.

The next couple of days must have been unbearable for Peter. When the rooster crowed, Peter's guilt fell on him like a two-ton truck. And the next day the rooster would again bring in the dawn with a fresh serving of regret and shame.

But by that third day, at the rising of the sun on the first Easter morning, even the rooster would be singing a different tune. That's because Easter is the true story of an empty tomb that fills the world. Jesus rising from the dead fills life with forgiveness, meaning, and purpose.

But at first, Jesus' friends and family didn't know what to think of the empty tomb. They thought it was the sign of the end. It was the opposite. It was a brand new beginning.

FINDING FORGIVENESS

On that Sunday morning two thousand years ago, a frantic Mary Magdalene found Peter and John on her way back from discovering the tomb was empty.

She came to them fearing the worst—that the Jewish religious leaders or the Roman officials had taken Jesus' body away. The disciples ran towards the garden where Jesus was buried.

John's Gospel points out that John outran Peter. But when Peter got there, he dashed right into the tomb. The cloths that had been wrapped round Jesus' body were there, but that was all. Maybe Mary was right that the body had been stolen?

But that idea was quickly overturned. Mary herself was the first to see Jesus alive. She immediately told the other disciples.

I wonder how Peter felt? His last shared memory with Jesus was the rooster crowing after his biggest failure. Now he had a chance to make new memories. But would Jesus want to see Peter? Would Jesus forgive him? Would Jesus still be Peter's friend?

Peter had seen Jesus offer forgiveness to the religious leader Nicodemus, to a rich young ruler, to a Samaritan woman with a questionable past, and to so many others. And even at the very end, with his last breaths, Jesus was still offering forgiveness, first to his executioners and finally to a criminal hanging on a cross next to him (Luke 23).

Would Jesus offer this same forgiveness to Peter? Peter knew he didn't deserve it. He may have thought it best to hide, despair, or just disappear. Maybe he should go back to his old life as a fisherman. Peter's thoughts and emotions had to be swirling inside him like a hurricane.

It can be easy to tell others how much God loves them and is willing to forgive them regardless of what they've done. It can be hard to believe that such grace is also available for us. That's because, in part, we know ourselves too well. We know something of the depths of our own sin. No matter how much we might try to fake it to others, we can't get away from ourselves.

Can Jesus love the *real* us?

The truth is, the real us is the only us with whom Jesus will do business. He won't settle for the fake us. That's because he really does love the real us. He died for the real us. He rose for the real us. Wonderfully, the real us is the one he's after.

THE SUNRISE BY THE SEA

In John's Gospel, Jesus appears to the disciples a couple of times after the resurrection. But we don't see any conversation between Jesus and Peter. If you want to see Jesus forgiving Peter, you have to wait until the very end. It's worth the wait.

For Peter, it ends much like it began. Jesus had found him fishing when he first called him. He told Peter he would make him a fisher of men (Matthew 4 v 18-19). In the same way that Peter was searching for fish, Jesus came to search for people who needed forgiveness. And Jesus called Peter to join him.

But now Peter was the one in need of finding. He was the one in need of forgiveness. And here we find Jesus looking for him. That's what Jesus does—he finds us when and where we need him most.

Just as when they had first met, Jesus stood on the lake shore watching Peter fish. Once Peter realized it was the Lord, he couldn't contain himself. He was too eager to wait for the boat to row in. So, he flung himself into the water and swam to meet Jesus, who had breakfast waiting on the shore.

Throughout the book we've examined this breakfast conversation between Jesus and Peter. It takes place after the worst chapter in Peter's life. He had three chances to confess his devotion to Jesus. But he struck out. Each time he denied that he even knew Jesus.

Peter is one of the greatest failures in all of the New Testament. That's one way to look at it.

Another way is that Peter's life is one of the greatest stories of forgiveness and restoration in the Bible. Peter went from saying he didn't know Jesus to not being able to shut up about Jesus. That's what grace can do in our lives.

Bob Goff puts it this way: "God finds us in the holes we dig for ourselves. We see failures; he sees foundations."

Peter hit rock bottom. And now Jesus was ready to start building.

But this wasn't the last time Peter would fail. We find at least one further example in Scripture. The apostle Paul had to confront Peter for refusing to eat with non-Jewish believers (Galatians 2 v 11-14). Peter was a disciple. He was an eyewitness of Jesus after the resurrection. Did he really need to be confronted about the sins of prejudice and cowardice?

Yep. On this side of the grave, all of us will need to be corrected from time to time. We fail to do the things we should do; we do the things we know we shouldn't (Romans 7 v 15). Does that sound familiar? The truth is, we all make a mess of things at times. Failure is in our future. But so is forgiveness.

MAKING IT PERSONAL

Like Peter, we have failed Jesus in our past. And like Peter, we aren't done failing yet. As one old hymn says, our hearts are prone to wander.

My friend Sam Allberry likes to say, "There is more forgiveness in Jesus than there is failure in us." But that can be so hard to believe, can't it? There can be a whole lot of failure in us, if we're honest. But since God knows everything, he knew what he was getting into with us from the very beginning. That means we can't surprise him.

That also means there will never be a moment in your Christian life when Jesus regrets forgiving you. There will never be a moment when you disgust him. That's because he knows you, the real you, and still he loves you, the real you. And his forgiveness is big enough for all of you—all of the real you.

We discover in the gospel that we can't hide: God knows us fully. We discover in Christ that we don't need to hide: God loves us deeply. This is the greatest news in the whole world.

Jesus never turns away anyone who's willing to admit they've messed up and need his help. The word in the Bible for this is repentance. It means agreeing with God that his way is best, saying we're sorry to him and others for how we've blown it, and recommitting to live for him in the future with his help.

Once you repent, the next step is to learn from your mistakes. While we won't have perfect obedience here on earth, there's certainly a lot we can learn from our failures. Choose a close friend who can keep you accountable, and think through the kinds of things that contributed to your failure. Make an action plan for how you want things to go differently in the future.

Maybe you feel like Peter—that you've blown it big time. Or instead of one massive mistake, perhaps you feel buried beneath a million bad decisions made over a long—too long—period of your life. Some readers might feel distanced from Jesus, not due to guilt-ridden decisions or deep-rooted habits but by a heart that's grown cold in the midst of doing good things. Or maybe you don't feel that you've blown it as such, but you know you could be more committed to living God's way in every part of your life. Like Peter, we all need to run to Jesus.

Recently I went kayaking on a large lake in northern Michigan. The lake was filled with islands and inlets—and surrounded by a whole lot of pine trees. No matter which way you looked, the shoreline looked the same.

I got lost. And when you're lost on a kayak, there's no quick way to find your way back. It's a slow process that involves a bit of patience and a whole lot of rowing.

After an exhausting couple of hours, I came around an island and noticed a peninsula that looked familiar. It was a very welcome sight. It was a youth camp that locals call "Presbyterian Point," and it is marked with a large white cross hanging from the rock edge.

After a couple hours of being lost, once I saw the cross I knew I could find my way home. The same is true for all of us. Forgiveness lies in one direction only. We'll find it at the cross. That doesn't mean our work is over, but it does mean we're heading in the right direction.

Wherever you are in your walk with God, look to the cross. That's where Jesus paid the ultimate price for our disobedience. The author of Hebrews tells us to throw off the sin that easily entangles us and to fix our eyes on

Jesus (Hebrews 12 v 1-2). By turning from our sin, we can enjoy a fresh start in our walk with God. By fixing our eyes on Jesus, we can begin to see the path forward in our fight to follow him.

It's God who gives us the desire to attempt to become more like Jesus.

So, trust God with both your successes and your failures. Becoming more like Jesus will be a messy ordeal. Some days it will be four steps forward. Some days it will be three steps back. Always keep in mind that one day Christ will return, and this struggle will finally be over. Praise God for that!

As long as there is a believing heart beating within your chest, God's love is big enough to take you back, his forgiveness strong enough to cover your faults, and his Spirit powerful enough to complete what God started in the first place. Don't let failure keep you from serving God. Peter didn't.

Jesus forgave Peter. He will forgive you too. Jesus used a failure like Peter. He can use you too.

OUTRO: TIME TO FACE THE DAY

*But grow in the grace and knowledge of our Lord and
Savior Jesus Christ. To him be glory both now and
forever! Amen.*
(Peter's final words from 2 Peter 3 v 18)

Losing your identity is a scary ordeal. I know. It just
happened to me.

I live in the middle of cornfields in Middle America, so
a speaking engagement in Florida was a rare chance to
see the beach. I had an amazing view of the ocean as I
sat next to the pool and started some editing work (on
this book). But later, as I grabbed a snack, someone else
grabbed my bag and quietly made off with it.

Thankfully they didn't get my laptop. What they did get
was my wallet, credit cards and driver's license, and the
keys for both my Florida rental car and my own car. The
thought that some stranger had my identification, credit
cards, and keys to my house and car sent me into a panic.

Everything worked out in the end, but losing your identity isn't fun. Cards are easy to cancel, but getting your identity back is a whole lot more work.

That's why identity security companies have popped up all over the place. And they all promise the same thing: to keep your personal life personal. After all, that's what we all want: to keep our identity under our control. It's frightening to think of someone else doing what they like with our identity.

WHAT'S IN YOUR WALLET?

I think some of us feel the same way about being a Christian. We want to keep our personal life personal, rather than hand it over to someone else—even someone as amazing as Jesus. Even though we have every reason to trust him, there's still that impulse to retain at least some control over our identity. Sure, we want to follow Jesus—but we also want to keep some level of control over our own lives.

I recently read a comment from a Christian brother on social media that says it well: "Feeling like I need to get serious about my purpose in Christ. Feeling scared about failing at it. Feeling afraid of giving over control of my life to the Lord. Feeling afraid of not giving over control to the Lord." Saying yes to Jesus means surrendering our identity to him.

That really can be scary. Following Jesus means relocating the center of our identity, from who we are and what we want to do to who Jesus is and what he wants to do through us. Who knows what it might cost us? Who knows where it might lead? Who knows? *God* knows. And he calls you to hand over your identity to him. He won't steal it.

This is at the heart of the breakfast conversation with Jesus. Peter's identity was about to be rocked. I'm not sure it would have been clear in the moment, but when you look at Peter's life, you see how different he became after this conversation with the risen Christ.

Transformation sometimes looks like this. It can look very normal. It can be nearly imperceptible at first. It might look like a breakfast meeting that slightly adjusts the direction of your life. Even if it looks really small to begin with, the further you get away from the place where you first shifted your direction, the more you'll realize the scope of the change.

Life is punctuated by these decisive moments that alter our direction. We sometimes miss them because we're focused on big calendar items, such as a graduation, a birthday, or a vacation. These things come. They go. Our expectation and enthusiasm builds and builds. And then, just like that, they're over. But in between these big items, there are quiet moments when we can make a step, even a small one, in a slightly different direction— a step that, in time, can dramatically affect our journey.

I think that's how this breakfast conversation was for Peter. He must have longed for Jesus to forgive him. This was the moment he had been looking forward to and desperately hoping would happen. But the morning after this conversation, he had to wake up and keep on with life.

No matter how powerful a moment—no matter the depth of inspiration or the joy of accomplishment—life just keeps moving, doesn't it?

But there are moments that leave their mark on us. There are times when something inside of us gets altered, something is edited, ideas get planted, dreams of what can be get imprinted, and slowly roots begin to grow. In time, this growth will mature and bear fruit.

THE LANDSCAPE OF CHANGE

Change often looks like that. It can look like nothing happens at all, not right at first. But deep on the inside, a small seed begins to disrupt the landscape of our lives. I pray that this conversation between Jesus and Peter could be like that for you.

Change doesn't always strike us with the force of a tsunami. This kind of change doesn't make the evening news. Not at first. Change is often more like a seed planted in a field by a farmer. Give it time. Water it. Let the sun do its thing. Eventually there will be a harvest.

Now, people notice a harvest. It's kind of an event. Often small towns in farming communities celebrate it with harvest festivals.

I live in a part of America like that: the Midwest. Our little town is surrounded by cornfields as far as the eye can see. When the harvest comes, it's obvious to everybody. You can't miss the tractors out at night in late summer or early fall, lights shining in the middle of the fields as farmers collect the fruit of their labor. There really is something beautiful about that.

What we don't notice is when the farmers plant the seeds. That's far less dramatic. No one around here has "planting festivals."

Planting may not be celebrated. Yet the soil conceals the secret: change is coming. A harvest is in the making. The harvest would never happen were it not for the uncelebrated and seemingly insignificant planting of seeds. That means, for us, that change—growth—is going to look a whole lot like work. Just ask a farmer.

Are you ready to be changed? Are you ready to do some work? It may take time for the harvest to grow, but the change in your heart is radical. It means saying to God, "Yes, I'm ready for you to change me. Please give me the courage to love you and follow you as I should. I know it may hurt. I'm sure there'll be times when I'd rather pull back. But I believe you want to change me and use me—*even me*—as you did Peter. And I'm excited to find out what that may look like."

I pray that seeds of change have been planted in your life from John 21. But know this: once you set your coffee cup and this book down, life isn't going to wait for you. So, get on with it.

DEVELOP A GROWTH TARGET

I want to offer some practical ideas for you to work toward your growth, knowing that "it is God who works in you to will and to act in order to fulfill his good purpose" (Philippians 2 v 13).

Think about your plan to grow as being like a target. Imagine a bullseye in the middle, surrounded by three concentric circles. You might even sketch out a target on a piece of paper or the back of a napkin to help you think through your growth plan. (We've provided a target on page 108 for those of you who find it difficult to draw circles.)

The center of the target, the bullseye, represents your personal relationship with God. You might start by writing the date to indicate that today you are committing to grow in your love for God. This may be the first time you've made this kind of promise to him, or you may be coming back to a level of love and commitment you felt some time back. Either way, today is a great day to commit your life more fully to the Lord.

Begin by spending some time today—now, or later today if necessary—getting alone and talking with God. Start by confessing sins. If you want these seeds to grow, you will have to begin by weeding the garden of your heart. Ask for God's help to overcome those things—bad things and good things alike—that you've allowed to become a greater priority than your love for him.

Don't rush this. This is important. Here are some really helpful thoughts from the American pastor and author A.W. Tozer to inform your time of confession with God:

> *Do a thorough job of repenting. Do not hurry to get it over with. Hasty repentance means shallow spiritual experience and lack of certainty in the whole of life. Let godly sorrow do her healing work. Until we allow the consciousness of sin to wound us, we will never develop a fear of evil. It is our wretched habit of tolerating sin that keeps us in our half-dead condition.*

Additionally, let this bullseye represent your daily commitment to spend time with God, reading his word and talking to him in prayer. Why not make this breakfast meeting a standing appointment on your calendar? It's through personal time with God that you will nurture and cultivate your heart for growth.

In the next circle, think through one or two people you plan to talk to about your growth plan—people who will pray for you and help you stick to your plan. They need to be people you trust and respect spiritually. They need to be those who will challenge you and commit to help you grow.

In the third circle, write the name of a local church you're connected with or that you plan to be connected with. As we discussed in chapter three, you can't grow in your love for God on your own. You can't say you love God but not love his people.

It's important for you to be involved in a church that believes and teaches the Bible. If you're already a part of a Bible-believing church, then great! If not, then finding one should be a top priority. This may be harder if there aren't many churches where you live, but you might start online looking for churches in your area that are clear in their view of Scripture. Visit a service and make an appointment with a leader to find out how you can get involved.

The last circle of the target might take a little more time, depending on where you are in your commitment to a local church. As we saw in chapter two, Jesus wants us to love him with a servant-like attitude. Jesus modeled his own servant heart in so many ways, not least of which was washing the disciples' feet at the last meal he shared with them.

In this last circle, write a few ways you want to serve God's people. How are you going to use your time, talents, and treasure in your local church? While we don't want to put serving God ahead of loving God, it is important that we learn to serve. As we serve God out of love for him and love for others, we will see even more growth in our own lives.

Once you've thought through this growth target, I encourage you to trust God for the harvest. While there is much work to be done, you will need to trust that in the soil of repentance, in the light of God's forgiveness, in the community of the church, and even in the field of this fallen world, a harvest can grow in your life. Change can happen. These small seeds of change can, in time, produce fruit.

You're not a lost project for God. You're not too far gone. He's bigger than your excuses. He's better than your sin. He's worthy of your life. And he's committed to finishing the work he started in you.

LIKE PETER...

Throughout the book we've examined the breakfast conversation from John 21. I'm convinced that if you sat down with Jesus, he would say some very similar things to you. Jesus asked Peter about his heart. *As with Peter*, Jesus wants us to love him. He wants our heart more than anything else.

Jesus spoke to Peter about his attitude of superiority—of claiming he was more loyal to Jesus than the other disciples. *As with Peter*, Jesus wants us to love him with humility. Instead of competing with one another, Jesus wants us to serve one another.

Each time Peter said he loved Jesus, Jesus commanded him to feed the sheep. *As with Peter*, Jesus wants us to care for his people, the church. We can't grow in our love for God without growing in our love for God's people. It's a package deal.

Then Jesus asked Peter to follow him even though it would cost him his life. Jesus had asked Peter to follow him three years earlier—and Peter had.

But following Jesus isn't a one-time event. It's a daily commitment. *As with Peter*, Jesus wants us to deny our own self-interests and pick up our cross to follow him regardless of where he leads. Sometimes that may be really tough. Sometimes it will be wonderful!

CLEARLY, DEARLY, AND NEARLY

This whole conversation took place after the worst failure in Peter's life. He had three chances to confess his devotion to Jesus on the night Jesus was arrested. But he struck out. Each time, he denied that he even knew Jesus. But at the end of Peter's life, his devotion to Jesus was as plain as day.

After faithfully serving God's people, Peter died as a martyr, just as Jesus had foretold. He was likely crucified in Rome under the bloody reign of Emperor Nero. The breakfast conversation he shared with Jesus came full circle. It was a breakfast conversation that changed his life.

It's my prayer that this last chapter of John's Gospel can set the stage for the next chapter of your life. It can, if you let it.

There's a prayer that's been passed down from the thirteenth century that provides a fitting conclusion to this book and an appropriate response to Jesus' invitation. May it be our prayer as well:

Thanks be to thee, my Lord Jesus Christ,
For all the benefits thou hast given me,
For all the pains and insults thou hast borne for me.
O most merciful Redeemer, Friend and Brother,
May I know thee more clearly,
Love thee more dearly,
And follow thee more nearly, day by day.
Amen.

GROWTH TARGET

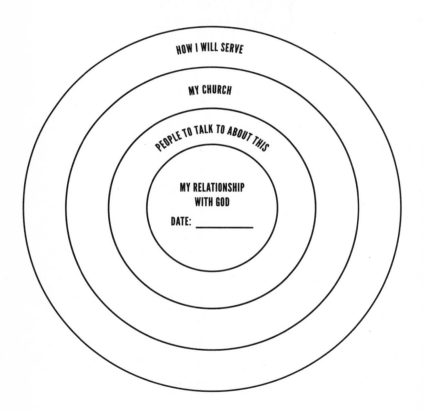

HOW I WILL SERVE

MY CHURCH

PEOPLE TO TALK TO ABOUT THIS

MY RELATIONSHIP
WITH GOD

DATE: _____

ONE-MONTH READING PLAN

DAY 1 John 1 v 1-28

DAY 2 John 1 v 29-51

DAY 3 John 2 v 1-25

DAY 4 John 3 v 1-36

DAY 5 John 4 v 1-42

DAY 6 John 4 v 43-54

DAY 7 John 5 v 1-15

DAY 8 John 5 v 16-47

DAY 9 John 6 v 1-24

DAY 10 John 6 v 25-71

DAY 11 John 7 v 1-24

DAY 12 John 7 v 25-53

DAY 13 John 8 v 1-30

DAY 14 John 8 v 31-59

DAY 15 John 9 v 1-41

DAY 16 John 10 v 1-21

DAY 17 John 10 v 22-42

DAY 18 John 11 v 1-57

DAY 19 John 12 v 1-19

DAY 20 John 12 v 20-50

DAY 21 John 13 v 1-38

DAY 22 John 14 v 1-31

DAY 23 John 15 v 1-27

DAY 24 John 16 v 1-15

DAY 25 John 16 v 16-33

DAY 26 John 17 v 1-26

DAY 27 John 18 v 1-40

DAY 28 John 19 v 1-16

DAY 29 John 19 v 17-42

DAY 30 John 20 v 1-31

DAY 31 John 21 v 1-25

THANK YOU

Many people leave their fingerprints on a book long before it's ever placed on the shelves of a store. No book is the sole product of any one individual. And for the Christian author, this is more intensely evident and should be more gratefully celebrated.

To my God: I want to give glory to God the Father for his marvelous grace, which alone is able to turn a fearful man like Peter into a powerful Pentecost preacher and, in the end, a faithful martyr. I want to give glory to God the Son for his compassionate dealings with highly flawed disciples like Peter, and like you and me. He is so kind! And I want to give glory to God the Spirit for filling us with power, pulling us out of the ruts, ditches, and holes we create for ourselves, and propelling us forward in pursuit of God's story for God's glory.

To my family: Many thanks to my wife, April, and our four children: Isaiah, Micah, Josiah, and Addilynn Joy. How much do I love you? Two much! How long will I love you?

Four ever! We might be crazy, but we got each other for this crazy life that is filled with crazy blessings from our amazing God. He is so good!

To my tribe: To Sam (Gamgee): thank you for your faithful friendship. To Dan and Jeff: D3 for life, whenever and wherever. To my Ohio posse: Anthony, Matt, Brian, Billy, and J.R., thanks for all your daily encouragement. To Dave, Barry, John, Blake, Jonathan, Eric, Gunner, Timothy, and Luke: I desperately miss working with a team like you guys. It was such a rare blessing to labor and laugh with you all.

To my publisher: There are a ton of people who are more worthy to write for you guys than me. Thank you for this, the third project, that we've worked on together. Alison, you are a consistent blessing. I'm proud to call you my editor and thankful to call you my friend.

Et al: Props to Jared Wilson, whose blog-post inspired my section about how God's grace is big enough for the real us, not the us hiding in the shadows. Shout out to Nate Pickowicz, who I totally forgot to properly acknowledge in my last book (oops). And thanks to Thomas White, for the encouragement and opportunities he's afforded me while at Cedarville to work on books like this one. Finally, thanks to Bob and Nicole at Maple Ridge Lodge, in Michigamme, Michigan, where I finished the edits for this book while enjoying your northern hospitality.

thegoodbook

COMPANY

BIBLICAL | RELEVANT | ACCESSIBLE

At The Good Book Company, we are dedicated to helping Christians and local churches grow. We believe that God's growth process always starts with hearing clearly what he has said to us through his timeless word—the Bible.

Ever since we opened our doors in 1991, we have been striving to produce Bible-based resources that bring glory to God. We have grown to become an international provider of user-friendly resources to the Christian community, with believers of all backgrounds and denominations using our books, Bible studies, devotionals, evangelistic resources, and DVD-based courses.

We want to equip ordinary Christians to live for Christ day by day, and churches to grow in their knowledge of God, their love for one another, and the effectiveness of their outreach.

Call us for a discussion of your needs or visit one of our local websites for more information on the resources and services we provide.

Your friends at The Good Book Company

thegoodbook.com | thegoodbook.co.uk
thegoodbook.com.au | thegoodbook.co.nz
thegoodbook.co.in